CAMBRIDGE TEXTS IN THE
HISTORY OF PHILOSOPHY

═══

PLATO
The Symposium

CAMBRIDGE TEXTS IN THE
HISTORY OF PHILOSOPHY

Series editors

KARL AMERIKS
Professor of Philosophy at the University of Notre Dame

DESMOND M. CLARKE
Professor of Philosophy at University College Cork

The main objective of Cambridge Texts in the History of Philosophy is to expand the range, variety, and quality of texts in the history of philosophy which are available in English. The series includes texts by familiar names (such as Descartes and Kant) and also by less well-known authors. Wherever possible, texts are published in complete and unabridged form, and translations are specially commissioned for the series. Each volume contains a critical introduction together with a guide to further reading and any necessary glossaries and textual apparatus. The volumes are designed for student use at undergraduate and postgraduate level and will be of interest not only to students of philosophy, but also to a wider audience of readers in the history of science, the history of theology, and the history of ideas.

For a list of titles published in the series, please see end of book.

PLATO

The Symposium

EDITED BY

M. C. HOWATSON
St. Anne's College, Oxford

FRISBEE C. C. SHEFFIELD
King's College, London

TRANSLATED BY

M. C. HOWATSON

CAMBRIDGE
UNIVERSITY PRESS

CAMBRIDGE
UNIVERSITY PRESS

University Printing House, Cambridge CB2 8BS, United Kingdom

Published in the United States of America by Cambridge University Press, New York

Cambridge University Press is part of the University of Cambridge.

It furthers the University's mission by disseminating knowledge in the pursuit of
education learning and research at the highest international levels of excellence

www.cambridge.org
Information on this title: www.cambridge.org/9780521864404

© Cambridge University Press 2008

First published 2008
3rd printing 2013

A catalogue record for this publication is available from the British Library

Library of Congress Cataloguing in Publication Data

Plato.
[Symposium. English]
Plato, the Symposium / edited by M. C. Howatson, Frisbee C. C. Sheffield ;
translated by M. C. Howatson.
p.   cm. – (Cambridge texts in the history of philosophy)
Includes index.
I S B N 978-0-521-86440-4 (hardback : alk. paper) – I S B N 978-0-521-68298-5
(pbk. : alk. paper)
I.   Love. I.   Howatson, M. C. II.   Sheffield, Frisbee C. C. (Frisbee Candida Cheyenne)
III.   Title.
B 385.A 5H 69 2008
184–dc22
2007051668

I S B N 978-0-521-86440-4 hardback
I S B N 978-0-521-68298-5 paperback

Contents

Introduction   *page* vii
Chronology   xxix
Further reading   xxxii
Translator's note   xxxiv

The Symposium ('The Drinking Party')   1

Glossary of Greek words   64
Glossary of names   70
Index of subjects   90

Introduction

Plato's writings are typically in the form of dialogues in which Socrates[1] (born 469 BC) discusses philosophical questions with other characters of his day.[2] Most of these are based on known historical figures, but the dialogues are not factual accounts; they are fictional, and often richly dramatic, products of Plato's philosophical imagination. The *Symposium* is a particularly dramatic work. It is set at the house of Agathon, a tragic poet celebrating his recent victory in 416 BC at one of the great dramatic festivals.[3] Those present are amongst the intellectual elite of the day. They include an exponent of heroic poetry (Phaedrus), an expert in the laws of various Greek states (Pausanias), a representative of medical expertise (Eryximachus), a comic poet (Aristophanes) and a philosopher (Socrates). The guests participate in a *symposium*,[4] a drinking party for aristocratic circles, on this occasion designed to honour Agathon's victory. Each guest delivers a speech in praise of *eros*, 'passionate love', or 'desire'.[5] The final speech is delivered by Alcibiades, a notorious associate of Socrates, who talks openly about his love for Socrates, in particular. The conversation is disrupted by a group of drunken revellers, but Socrates continues to talk way into the night as he tries to persuade Aristophanes and Agathon that

---

[1] For all names, such as Socrates here, see Glossary of names.

[2] Plato was born sometime in the 420s.

[3] Although we know Agathon did win a theatrical competition in 416 BC, and that the guests are real historical figures, there is no historical evidence for a celebration of the sort Plato describes in the *Symposium*. The work itself is believed to have been composed sometime between 385 BC and 370 BC. For discussion of the date of composition, see H. Mattingly 'The date of Plato's *Symposium*', *Phronesis* (1958) 3: 31–9 and K. Dover 'The date of Plato's *Symposium*', *Phronesis* (1965) 10: 2–20.

[4] Symposium literally means 'drinking together'.

[5] For all Greek terms mentioned in the Introduction, such as *eros* here, see Glossary.

the same author should be able to compose both comedy and tragedy. The events of this gathering are retold some years later by Apollodorus, another Socratic intimate, whose love for Socrates has led him to memorise the entire occasion by heart.

The dramatic aspects of this work are not limited to the lively setting and rich characterisation. During the time between Agathon's drinking party and its recollection by Apollodorus, the Athenians had lost some of the confidence shown here by Agathon and his peers. Just a year after Agathon's victory, Alcibiades had persuaded the Athenians to embark on the doomed Sicilian expedition. The Athenian defeat here marked a turning point in an already bitter struggle with Sparta (the Peloponnesian War). Two religious scandals also took their toll: the so-called profanation (i.e. parodying) of the sacred Mysteries and the mutilation of the herms.[6] Since those involved in this desecration were from the Athenian aristocracy, it was widely held that the perpetrators were trying to undermine the democratic government. One of these events was believed to have been committed by a group of rowdy symposiasts after an event much like Agathon's symposium described here, and amongst those accused of involvement were Alcibiades and Phaedrus and very possibly Eryximachus. The inclusion of these figures at a dialogue set at a symposium, and the recollection of this occasion after these events had already occurred, invites the reader to consider these characters on the brink of their impending tragedy. The lives and loves they reveal in their speeches may well be Plato's contribution to a post-war debate about such matters.

Eros and education

The speeches about *eros* each make a very distinctive contribution to an understanding of the nature of human desire and the aim of loving relationships. Although this topic may not be prominent with many philosophers today, nor setting their work at a drinking party, these features of this lively dialogue will, in fact, take us deep into the serious business of Plato's ethics. Among members of the Athenian elite during the fifth and fourth centuries relationships between an older male lover (*erastes*) and a younger male beloved (*eromenos*) were not uncommon. Typically in such relationships an older partner sought sexual favours from a youth on the

---

[6] See Glossary of names for details of these events.

verge of manhood in return for providing social, political and moral training. The feelings of desire and, at best, concern for the welfare of one's partner were employed for the socially productive end of furthering the education of the young.[7] An important context for such relationships was the Greek symposium, such as the one that forms the setting for this dialogue. Although symposia were places to indulge in the physical pleasures of food, drink and sex, they were also a place to cultivate the pleasures of the mind. After dinner, with lover and beloved reclining on the same couch, lovers would sing drinking songs, or recite poetry or prose, to their beloveds. The content would often reflect on the practices of those gathered at the symposium, and how they should eat, drink and desire in the right way. The topic of this dialogue was, in fact, already an established theme in a context that was concerned with both arousing, and regulating, desires.[8]

The fact that erotic relationships had this educational dimension, and that the symposium was an important forum for such relationships, goes some way towards explaining why Plato wrote this dialogue. As we might expect from a philosopher whose works consistently focus on the nature of the good life and how it is achieved, Plato will have much to say here also about the sorts of values that lovers should transmit to their beloveds as they pass the wine cup. Since it is on the basis of a certain conception of a flourishing life that certain sorts of things are advocated to the young as valuable, the dialogue explores the nature of *eudaimonia*, which may be translated as happiness or flourishing. This is ultimately why a dialogue devoted to the nature of erotic relationships is at its core an ethical work, which culminates in the specification of 'the life which a human being should live' (211d). And it is this concern that relates the *Symposium* to a fundamental question that informs a variety of Platonic dialogues: how should one live (cf. *Gorgias* 500c; *Republic* 352d)?

---

[7] On pederasty as an important social institution in classical Athens, see Dover (1978); Bremmer (1990).

[8] On the educational function of the symposium, see Bremmer (1990) 135–49; Calame (1999) 93–101. See also Hunter (2004) 6, who argues that 'from an early date the literature of the symposium frequently involves a meta-discourse upon the conduct of the symposium itself; the overriding interest in their own procedures which characterises many members of modern clubs and societies found an ancient counterpart in sympotic reflections upon symposia, and Plato's *Symposium* is to be seen within an evolving fourth century tradition of prose *sympotika*, which look back to the sympotic poetry of the archaic period'.

Plato's concern with desire and its role in the good life in a number of works suggests that he believed that one's ability to act well and to lead a worthwhile and good life depends, in part, on desiring the right kinds of things and acting on that basis. What, or whom, one desires determines the choices one makes and thereby affects one's chances of leading a worthwhile and happy life. Consider, for example, the behaviour at the start of the dialogue of Apollodorus, who proudly announces that his life has been re-orientated towards the love of wisdom. Pursuing this particular goal, he believes, will lead to the kind of happiness simply unavailable to those whose lives are orientated towards the pursuit of wealth (173a). In the speeches Plato will be considering a variety of things thought to be worthy of desire and pursuit, and at the heart of the dialogue stands Socrates' argument for the centrality of philosophy to the happy human life (*philo-sophia*, means literally 'the love of wisdom'). The fact that desires are seen to play such an important role in the good life locates this text amongst many other ancient works concerned with the development of character and how that contributes to a good human life.[9]

An overview of the speeches

The *Symposium* consists mainly of a series of praise speeches (*encomia*). In some respects this is a departure from the usual form of Plato's dialogues, which are typically characterised by a question and answer format. In many of these works Socrates is pitted against some contemporary figure whose claims to wisdom he examines and refutes by a particular technique of questioning, often referred to as an *elenchus*, an examination, or refutation. In the *Symposium* we see a more constructive Socrates delivering an extended speech along with his peers.[10] Since each speaker attempts to outdo his predecessor, the dialogue can still be seen as combative in nature and, with Socrates' speech occupying centre stage, the centrality of philosophy to a proper understanding of the topic is made clear. But although Socrates maintains his critical distance from his peers in this dialogue (198b–199b), the previous speeches need not be read as extraneous to the

---

[9] This 'agent-centred' rather than 'act-centred' approach, as it has come to be known, has been revived in recent times as virtue ethics has become more popular. This approach emphasises the motives and character of moral agents, as opposed to duties or rules (deontology), or consequences of action (consequentialism).

[10] His speech is actually a reported dialogue with a priestess called Diotima.

philosophical core of the work. They play a significant role by providing the reader with a sense of the agreements and disagreements on the subject, and by clarifying the sorts of puzzles that a clear and explanatory account – of the sort that Socrates professes to deliver (198b) – must resolve.[11]

For example, Phaedrus (178a–180b), the first speaker, puts the issue of the role of love in moral education firmly on the agenda. He argues that a love relationship has the greatest power when it comes to acquiring excellence (*arete*) and happiness, as he conceives of such things (180b). In the presence of one's lover one is inspired to pursue honour and thereby to perform noble deeds, such as acts of heroism. Although the idea that loving relationships bring out the best in one may help to explain the positive effects of love, it is unclear why a love of honour, rather than pleasure, say, is fostered by such relationships. Do all lovers arouse this aim, or just lovers of a certain sort?

Pausanias (180c–185c) builds on Phaedrus' idea that a proper love relationship leads to the acquisition of some sort of excellence (*arete*, 185b). Since he believes that cultivating wisdom is crucial here (184d), he argues that attraction to a person's soul (*psuche*) in particular will encourage the development of that soul and its characteristic excellences. This account, at least, raises the important point that if we are to understand the sort of relationship that can contribute to the good life, then we need an account of the sort of excellence that is central to that life. If wisdom is intimately related to human excellence, as Pausanias states, then we can grasp why a beneficial relationship is focused on the development of the soul. Some kind of account remains to be given of just what sort of wisdom will lead to such benefits and why, and who might be its best exponent.

---

[11] Since Plato does not appear in *propria persona* in the work, or endorse explicitly the views of the character Socrates, one might question whether Socrates' speech does mark the philosophical core of the work, as I have suggested. Perhaps Socrates should be considered as one voice amongst many in the work, with none of the characters carrying more authorial authority than any other. If so, then perhaps each should be given equal weight in our reading. Since the dialogue begins and ends with Socratic devotees, and Socrates' speech is by far the longest and most complex, it is difficult not to read the dialogue with the Socrates character occupying centre stage. Moreover, many of his views here coincide with views argued for elsewhere in the Platonic dialogues. This suggests that, at the very least, Socrates' speech expresses some of Plato's enduring philosophical preoccupations. Whether these are considered to be Platonic doctrine expressed through a Socratic mouthpiece is a further question, however. For a general discussion of the difficulties of extracting doctrine from Plato's works, see M. Frede (1992) and for a defence of a doctrinal approach, see J. Beversluis (2006).

Eryximachus (186a–188e) addresses this issue next. He agrees with Phaedrus and Pausanias that the aim of a beneficial love relationship is the cultivation of some kind of human excellence (188d), and adds that the correct lover must have an expertise. One can see how this suggestion arises naturally from the focus on the development of the soul highlighted by Pausanias. Since Eryximachus construes good order as essential for excellence, he advocates the expertise of the doctor whose main concern, he explains, is with harmonising (i.e. ordering) the various elements of the body. Why this should be relevant to the good order of the soul is not so clear, however.

Aristophanes (189c–193d) raises a new issue. He claims that in order to appreciate why love has such a beneficial impact on human life we need an account of human nature and its needs. According to this account, human beings are needy creatures who strive towards a state of self-realisation and happiness. Love aims at the completion of self, and lovers seek someone akin to themselves who can make them complete and whole (193d). Although it seems plausible to claim that an account of the beneficial effects of love must begin from an account of human nature and its needs, Aristophanes' account of these needs, and how they can best be satisfied, also raises questions. As Socrates puts it later, we are willing to cut off our own hands and feet if they are diseased (205e), and therefore the aim of human desire cannot be limited to things that are akin to us.

According to Agathon (194e–198a), the previous speakers have failed to explain the sort of nature responsible for the benefits praised (195a). Since 'no one could teach or impart to another an art he does not know or possess himself' (196e), lovers must themselves be in every way supremely beautiful and virtuous if they are to confer such benefits on others (196b). Lovers pursue, and produce, beautiful and fine things and induce others to create such things e.g. wisdom, construed here as poetic skill (196d–e). Although it seems plausible to claim that there is something creative about desire, the puzzle that arises specifically from this account is why this is the case. If lovers are already in possession of almost all the good things one could imagine (as Agathon supposes), then why do they engage in such creative endeavour at all, or inspire anyone else to do the same?

Although the speeches stand in their own right as inventive, and often rhetorically brilliant, display pieces appropriate to Agathon's victory banquet, they also help us to realise just what is involved in providing a clear and consistent explanation of the nature of love. We might agree with the speakers, for example, that happiness (*eudaimonia*) plays a central role in a positive account of love. We might also agree that love can contribute towards the cultivation of various sorts of excellence, and that this has something to do with pursuing beauty. But there is a vast spectrum of different ideas available about the nature of happiness, and what constitutes human excellence and, consequently, who are the best lovers. In one account bravery on the battlefield is the privileged value and this is somehow related to a love of honour (Phaedrus). In another, wisdom is central to excellence (Pausanias). Eryximachus prizes the virtue of the doctor, or seer, who can promote a harmonious order (188d). Aristophanes highlights the virtues of the politician (192a), and Agathon gives priority to poetic skill (196d). If we are to understand why *eros* is a fitting subject for praise at all, then what stands in need of explanation is some account of which of these pursuits (if any) are central to *eros* and why, and what relationship holds between their pursuit and happiness.

Socrates' speech[12]

Since Socrates claims to provide an account that privileges the truth over rhetorical effect (198b), we expect an attempt to resolve such puzzles. His speech is, at least, systematic. First, he provides an account of the nature of desire (203b), he then proceeds to its aims (204d), and finally he outlines its characteristic activity (206b), the most central of which, he argues, is philosophy (210–212).[13] Socrates argues that the highest form of *eros* is contemplation of the Beautiful itself, an abstract and perfect idea of beauty. Happiness resides in intellectual union with this idea. This is a claim that has led to accusations of 'cold-hearted egoism' from critics who suppose that Plato fails here to appreciate something distinctively human about love.[14] To allow for better scrutiny of what is arguably the central idea of the work let us first give it some context by piecing together the various strands of Socrates' speech.

[12] The bulk of the speech is ostensibly by the priestess Diotima. See Glossary, and Sheffield (2006), chapter 2.

[13] His procedure suggests that he believes that it is only when one has correctly identified the nature of one's subject matter that one can go on to make inferences about its effects. This procedure can be compared to those dialogues in which Socrates prioritises answers to his 'What is X?' question. This is often referred to as 'the priority of definition'. See, for example, *Meno* 71b3–4.

[14] This charge was initially brought by Gregory Vlastos (1981). See further below.

The nature of desire (199d–204c)

Socrates argues that Agathon was mistaken to suppose that lovers are beautiful and fulfilled creatures. If they were in such a state then there would be no reason for them to desire such things as beauty. Nor are they in a state of complete deficiency, however. If they were completely deficient creatures then they would not even be aware of their need of such things, nor strive to remedy a lack they fail to perceive. Consider the case of ignorance. Those who are completely stupid are not even aware that they lack wisdom, and so do not search for it, whilst those in possession of knowledge do not search for what they already possess. Lovers of wisdom are those who are in between a state of lack and possession (204b). In more general terms, lovers are those who are aware of a lack of the beautiful and good things they desire (whatever these may be), and who strive towards the possession of those things. In response to obvious counter-examples, such as cases where one appears to desire something one already possesses (e.g. health), Socrates argues that in such cases what one, in fact, desires is the possession of these things in the future. Since this future state of affairs is not something one currently possesses, such cases can also be considered to be examples of desiring something for which there is a perceived lack.[15]

The aim of desire (204d–206b)

Why desiring agents typically strive for something good and beautiful that they lack is addressed next. Desire, Socrates argues, occurs for the sake of something (204d). When we desire something we are aiming at the attainment of some goal. Although it seems axiomatic amongst all the speakers that beauty is the object of desire, Socrates is initially unclear as to what goal a desiring agent aims for in that pursuit. When he considers the good as an object, though, he is able to see more clearly the goal for the sake of which the agent acts: happiness. Happiness, he argues, is the end of human desire (its *telos*); for unlike other desirable ends, no one would ask why one wants to achieve *that* (205a1–3). In this rather laboured portion of the account Socrates is making a substantive point. It is that when we consider what it is that we desire (e.g. sex, or money, or wisdom), we can

---

[15] It was Aristophanes who highlighted first the centrality of lack in our experience of desire.

think about how our desires relate to further ends (e.g. the pursuit of pleasure or knowledge), and discover what is of most importance to us (e.g. happiness). There is, Socrates supposes, an end, or a greatest good, towards which our desires and actions ultimately aim.[16] What we really want as desiring agents is the possession of the sort of good that will satisfy our desire for happiness. This reflection suggests to Socrates that people are mistaken to suppose that *eros* refers to sexual desire exclusively; in fact, it is happiness quite generally that is desired and sexual desire is just one way (a pretty poor way, he will argue) in which this broader aim is manifested (205a).

This claim is often seen as part of a larger Platonic thesis referred to as *psychological eudaimonism*, which occurs in other Platonic dialogues. This thesis claims that we desire something if and only if we believe that it will contribute to our overall happiness (whether or not we are mistaken). When we go astray, this is not because there is something wrong with our desires (for our own good and happiness), but because of some cognitive deficiency on our part (failure to identify correctly the nature of this good). This thesis has been criticised for what is often termed its intellectualism, according to which people act in what they perceive to be their best interests. This seems to ignore the fact that people often pursue things that are bad for them. Reflecting on how to interpret Socrates' position most charitably might begin by probing the nature of such apparently bad desires. An often cited example is smoking. If a cigarette (a bad thing) is desired, but the description under which it is desired is as a good thing (e.g. as a pleasure inducer rather than as a cancer inducer), is this a counter-example to *psychological eudaimonism*?[17] When we desire such apparently bad things are we, in fact, pursuing them as such? Do we ignore (deliberately or otherwise) the aspects of the desired thing that will cause us harm? If so, are such cases genuine counter-examples to Socrates' claim? Reflection often shows that it is difficult to find cases where one desires something bad that is known to cause overall harm and misery, and that the thing in question is still desired as such.

Even if one concedes this, however, one might agree that there are *some* desires that are sensitive to considerations of this kind but object that there are others that are entirely independent of such thoughts. In other

---

[16] Cf. *Symposium* 204e–205a with *Euthydemus* 278e–282a and *Philebus* 20b–23a, 60a–61a.
[17] Arguments at *Meno* 77a–78a are particularly helpful in this context.

works (e.g. the *Republic*) Plato explored aspects of human motivation that operate independently of any consideration about the value of its desired ends. In the *Symposium*, consideration is limited to desires for our own good and happiness. This has led some scholars to suppose that the *Symposium* operates with a rather simplistic, intellectualist, psychology that fails to account for the complexity of human motivation (e.g. non-rational desires). But caution is required when interpreting Socrates' claims in the *Symposium*. Socrates does not, in fact, claim that all *desire* (*epithumia*) is directed towards the acquisition of good things and happiness, but that all *eros* is so directed (205d). He is only committed to the claim that *eros* is that area of desire concerned with the acquisition of good things and happiness. It may well be the case that there are other desires (more basic appetitive ones, that might better be called drives, e.g. hunger), that are not instances of *eros*, nor thereby of a broad desire for good things and happiness.[18] If so, then we are not entitled to draw general inferences about Socrates' views on the nature of desire as such in the *Symposium*. This is a dialogue about the human aspiration towards happiness, and how that desire is best satisfied. Whether such desires are the only ones Plato entertained at this point in his career is a further issue, not easily settled on the basis of the evidence of the *Symposium*.

One thing that is clear is why Socrates' account will move from an analysis of the nature of such desire to an account of knowledge and its acquisition; for if we all have a desire for our own good and happiness, the issue becomes how to identify correctly the nature of this good. Talk of correctly identifying a good we consider to be central to our happiness might sound rather odd to a modern reader, though. Happiness is quite often conceived as a subjective state to be determined from the inside, so to speak. If happiness is the sort of thing that individuals decide upon for themselves on the basis of how they feel at any given moment, for example, then how can philosophical analysis determine whether or not we are happy? This highlights the difficulties in translating *eudaimonia* as 'happiness'. *Eudaimonia* was considered not just to be a subjective feeling of pleasure, or contentment, or the mere satisfaction of an individual's desires (whatever these may be). What is under consideration here is whatever it is that makes a life worthwhile, that is, the success, or flourishing, of a human being who can be considered to be living well.

---

[18] There is a range of different desire terms employed in this text (*eros, epithumia* and *boulesis*).

Whether or not an individual is flourishing is more plausibly something about which one can be wrong, and which can be subjected to philosophical scrutiny. What counts as a flourishing human life, and on what basis one decides that issue, are further, difficult, questions. Socrates' argument for the superiority of the philosophical life will stand, or fall, by the plausibility of his criteria for deciding the issue (for which see below).

Socrates' assumption that there is some one good we seek as central to the happy life also deserves some reflection. He instances moneymaking, athletics and philosophy (205d).[19] It is not clear why one would pursue a single good of this kind rather than choose a rich variety of different goods in one's life. Nor is it clear how, if at all, this good might function with other valuable things in a flourishing life. The behaviour of Apollodorus at the start of the dialogue provides one model for thinking about such things. Before reciting his recollection of Agathon's banquet he explains that he used to run around all over the place before he discovered the pleasures of philosophy (173a). The implication is that his newfound valuation of wisdom has given his life an organised and focused structure. If the good functions in some way like this, that need not mean that one pursues one thing to the exclusion of all others. It might mean only that this good is the value one chooses to maximise and which one uses to adjudicate competing claims on one's time and attention. It is a real question how Socrates will end up conceiving of the good, and whether he advocates what is often referred to as an inclusive conception of the good which involves valuing other good things, or an exclusive conception which forsakes other goods in favour of one value.

The claim that happiness (however conceived) is the real end of desire has consequences for the rest of the account. For the good that will satisfy that desire will be a good of a certain sort. It will be the sort of thing that is desired for its own sake, for example; for we never want happiness for the sake of any further end. Socrates also suggests that it will be an enduring good: he says that we want immortality with the good (207a). These can be taken to be the criteria for judging competing conceptions of happiness.

---

[19] Socrates considers the desires for honour (208c) and wisdom (211c) in what he calls the Lower and Higher Mysteries of love. It is an interesting question why Socrates calls the final section of his account 'the Higher Mysteries' (and so, by implication, the previous section 'the Lower Mysteries'), after the religious Mysteries presumably (for which see Glossary of names under 'Mysteries'). This is perhaps partly explained by the fact that the real end of love is (a) something divine, and (b) a mystery to most lovers who fail to achieve this end.

Now, whilst we might concede that rational agents desire their own happiness, and even that there is a single, dominant, good that is central to that happiness, many readers will be stumped as to why we are also thought to desire immortality with this good. Again, reflection on the kind of good in question may be helpful here. If we keep in mind that *eudaimonia* is not conceived as a state of felicity, or a transitory feeling of pleasure or contentment, but as whatever it is that makes one's life a worthwhile and flourishing one, then perhaps it is the case that whatever good we take to be central to our happiness must be the kind of good that is possessed in a lasting way if it is to be the right kind of good at all. What constitutes *eudaimonia* is not to be had in a moment in time. Even if we concede this, though, we are still left with little explanation for why this desire is thought by Socrates to extend beyond a lifespan. Is this just wanton hyperbole? There are different ways to interpret this claim. There might be some goods with which one identifies to such an extent that their survival entails one's own, even though one's body has ceased to live. Consider the flourishing of one's children, for example, or the realisation of treasured projects one knows will unfold only after one's death. It seems that people engage quite often in valuable pursuits they know will come to fruition only after their death, hoping perhaps that something good with which they identify will endure beyond their lifespan. Or perhaps the desire for immortality with the good is a desire for a certain quality of existence which typically (for a Greek) characterised the divine. It may well be the case that different desiring agents have different notions of how to achieve their share of the divine. The plausibility of this idea will depend upon the sort of good Socrates advocates as central to the happy life.

The characteristic activity of desire (206b–208b)

According to Socrates this pursuit of good things and happiness manifests itself in a very particular way because of certain aspects of our mortal nature. As Aristophanes had already intimated, human beings are needy creatures whose happiness is not a given state of the soul. In other words, we are not (like gods) just born happy, but we need to *create* a good life for ourselves. This dynamic tendency is built into the very fabric of our survival. Consider the variety of dynamic activities involved in maintaining a mortal life and preserving it from change and loss, for example: we need nutritional replenishment to maintain our hair and skin, and mental practices of various kinds to retain knowledge (207d–208b). The desire for good things and happiness typically manifests itself in some form of activity because mortal beings need to create a certain sort of good life for themselves. This explains why Agathon was right to think that desire is typically productive in a broad sense.

Through a strange set of images, Socrates describes the endeavours through which we try to achieve good things and happiness by claiming that we are all pregnant in body and soul, and that we desire to express that pregnancy in an encounter with beauty (206b).[20] Some people are drawn towards physical beauty and produce children (an expression of a physical pregnancy) in the hope that these will secure them a memory and happiness (208e), whilst others are drawn towards cities and souls in which they can be productive of 'manifold virtue' (expressions of a psychic pregnancy) including acts of heroism (208d), lawmaking (209d), poetic displays (209a), political leadership (209a) and educational conversations (209b). Such virtuous productivity is designed to secure something good – honour in this case – for their producers, in the form of cults or shrines set up as memorials (208c, 209e). This is why, Socrates explains, desire is not of the beautiful, as he puts it (206e), but of production in a beautiful environment; it is the good things that result from an encounter with beauty that promise happiness. Since productive activity in a beautiful environment is the only way in which mortal beings can achieve a share of happiness (208b), this explains why creative activity of various kinds is the characteristic way in which human desire manifests itself.[21]

---

[20] The claim that all human beings are pregnant in body and soul may simply be a way of indicating that human beings have certain natural abilities, or potentialities: for children in the physical case and for wisdom and other excellences in the case of the soul (209a3).

[21] The fact that it is beauty that presides over our attempts to secure good things and happiness shows that it is closely related to the good, though the precise nature of this relationship is controversial. Beauty appears to be pursued in each case because it is a visible manifestation of something good and, as lovers of the good, beauty thereby prompts us to secure some good for ourselves. Consider the case of Socrates and his devotees, for example. Socrates' beauty resides in his ability to show them the wisdom they lack, and perceive to be of value (175d, 219d, 222a). In so doing, his beauty prompts them towards a good they desire, and it provides an appropriate environment for them to procure that value for themselves; for intellectual intercourse with Socrates is conducive to the attainment of wisdom. In this way our response to beauty is indicative of what we value and, as such, it can draw us into the good life. This was a theme Plato was to explore in the *Republic*.

The best expression of desire (210a–212b)

Socrates moves on to describe a very particular pursuit of beauty in what is arguably the most famous section of the work: the 'ascent of desire', so-called because it describes a series of attractions to a hierarchy of beautiful objects. It is here that he claims that the best expression of desire is contemplation of an abstract and perfect Idea of Beauty. Socrates describes an encounter with a variety of different beautiful objects that culminates in the acquisition of wisdom about the real nature of beauty itself. The manner of this desiring agent's response to beauty suggests that there is a very particular kind of desire at work here – philosophical desire. For this pursuit of beauty is characterised by *thinking* about what is similar about a variety of different beautiful objects and focusing on that common quality (210b).[22] First one reflects upon the beauty of bodies, then the beauty of souls, and laws, practices and various branches of knowledge, until finally, if successful, one can apprehend what beauty is, in its essential nature. The object of this apprehension is a purely intelligible object, grasped, if at all, by the intellect: the Idea, or Form, of Beauty. This beautiful object has a stable nature, it is immune from change of any kind, and it admits of no imperfections. In this it differs from the perceptible beautiful things we experience, which are subject to change over time, appear beautiful to one person and not to another, and whose natures are beautiful in one respect but not in another. Although defective in this way, these beautiful things share in the nature of this Form and, to the extent that they do so, reflection on the common feature of these beautiful things can lead to the apprehension of this Form. If one pursues beauty in this reflective way, according to Socrates, then one is able to contemplate the Beautiful itself, and to produce a genuine good: knowledge about beauty (211d) and true virtue (212a). As one needs physical union to produce physical offspring in physical beauty, so one needs intellectual engagement of this kind to encounter an intelligible beauty and produce an intellectual offspring of this sort.

There are some substantial ideas behind this dense passage and not all of them are argued for in the *Symposium* itself. What exactly is the relationship between the knowledge acquired here and the virtue and happiness which, Socrates argued earlier, are the true goals of *eros*? Why

---

[22] Such progress shares features in common with Socrates' search for the *eidos* – the essential feature of a thing – that is common to many other dialogues.

should knowledge concern an abstract object of this kind? Why suppose that there are such things as Forms, or that beauty is homogeneous across a range of cases, in such a way that reflection upon beautiful bodies and souls, for example, can lead to a unified understanding of this Form? What reasons do we have for accepting this, or for thinking that there is anything over and above the perceptible examples of this property? Arguments for some of these claims are lacking in the *Symposium*.

Before tackling the vexed question of the relationship between knowledge and virtue and happiness, let us start with the nature of the knowledge acquired here. In other dialogues Plato expresses doubts about the ability of the perceptible world to deliver knowledge. Some philosophers before him (e.g. Heraclitus) held that the perceptible world was in a state of constant flux and change. If knowledge is the sort of thing that is stable and unerring, then it cannot be of perceptible, changeable things. Either there is no such knowledge, or it is to be had elsewhere. Plato was no sceptic. Since he believed in the possibility of stable knowledge, he supposed that the objects of such knowledge were changeless and perfect intelligible objects – the Forms. Such ideas are implicit in the *Symposium*. The distinctive characteristics of the Form of Beauty are conveyed by means of a derogatory contrast with perceptible beautiful things. Whereas the form is stable, immune from change and uniform, the things that share in the nature of this form are unstable and changeable, and exhibit opposite characteristics in the manner discussed above (211a–b). As such, we suppose, they will yield only a confused and changeable grasp of the nature of beauty. If knowledge is the sort of thing that is unerring, true at all times, and to all (capable) perceivers, then such a thing cannot be grounded in a grasp of the sensible things experienced in the world. It must be had, if at all, by grasping the relevant Form.[23]

If Socrates holds such abstract metaphysical views about the nature of knowledge, then we can appreciate why an account of the acquisition of knowledge leads to the grasp of a Form. What may not be so clear is why the account leads to the acquisition of such knowledge in the first place, and what relationship holds between the acquisition of this knowledge and virtue, or the human good. If the aim of *eros* is the possession of the sort of good that will satisfy a desire for happiness, then what is it about

---

[23] The presence of Forms suggests that the *Symposium* is a middle-period work, perhaps close in date to the *Republic*, where this theory finds fuller expression. For the role of this theory in Plato's account of knowledge, see G. Fine (2003).

this kind of knowledge that will deliver that? Now, one might suppose that the pursuit of happiness is inextricably linked to an understanding of what is good for us; for without such knowledge we will be unable to make the sort of choices that will benefit us. One might also think that reflection on what makes bodies and souls into *beautiful* bodies and souls (in the manner of the desiring agent in the ascent) contributes to an understanding of what makes a fine and beautiful (in the moral sense) human being. But Socrates' account suggests rather more than the notion that such knowledge contributes to virtue. His claim is not that virtue requires knowing about what makes beautiful bodies and souls into instances of their kind, so that one could go out into the world and exercise that knowledge in some virtuous activity of one sort or another. Rather, his claim appears to be that the activity of contemplating the Form of Beauty is itself a virtuous activity. 'There is the life', we are told, 'which a human being should live, in the contemplation of Beauty itself' (211d). Since nothing further is required to produce true virtue, it is strongly suggested that to contemplate the Idea of Beauty just is to cultivate a certain kind of – intellectual – virtue.[24] And if this is 'the life which a human being should live', it is also suggested that this particular virtue is sufficient for happiness.[25]

So Socrates' account of our desire for the good concludes by discussing the nature of knowledge and its acquisition for the following reason. Virtue is assumed here, as it was in the previous speeches, to be good for its possessor (virtue is not conceived to be something separate from the flourishing of the human being), and this good resides in a certain kind of intellectual activity – the contemplation of the Form of Beauty. If so, why is this intellectual activity considered to be the best good, and more central to human happiness than any of the other excellences mentioned? It is questionable whether Socrates has established sufficiently robust criteria against which one can assess the supposed superiority of contemplation. The earlier remarks about the nature of happiness as the proper end of human desire were very suggestive, however (205aff.). We learnt there

---

[24] I am here taking it that the activity of contemplating and that of producing true virtue are one and the same activity. For further arguments for this claim see Sheffield (2006) 134.

[25] This need not be taken to imply that philosophical desire shows no concern for other persons. At 202e Socrates explains that Eros personified – and so, by implication, human desire – moves from the human to the divine *and* from the divine to the human realm. This may be taken to suggest that it is part of the proper functioning of desiring agents that they go back from contemplation of the divine Form (211e) to the world of human concerns. See page xvii and below xxv with footnote 31.

that happiness is a final good (a *telos*) – not desired for the sake of a further end. If so, then the attainment of whatever good we take to be central to our happiness must also be a final good that is desired for its own sake if it is to satisfy this desire. Further, as he also adds, it must be possessed in an enduring way; we want such a good 'always'. The account of the Higher Mysteries of desire, which describe the philosophical ascent to the Form, is one in which the notion of a real end of desire – a *telos* – looms large. If contemplation of the Idea of Beauty is 'that for the sake of which' all desire aims, and occupies a position in the Highest Mysteries of love because it is the real end of human desire, this must be because it is the sort of good that will satisfy our desire for happiness.

It is not altogether clear why this is the case. The desiring agents Socrates considers in the so-called Lower Mysteries (209c–210a) are the main figures of comparison here, and they are distinguished from the desiring agents of the Higher Mysteries (210a–212b) in at least two ways: they pursue a different kind of beauty, and they desire a different kind of good (honour, 208c).[26] The metaphysics of Forms discussed earlier is part of Socrates' attack on their pursuit of beauty. The desiring agents of the Lower Mysteries pursue perceptible, sensible, beautiful things, such as beautiful boys, or cities in which to be productive educators, or lawgivers. Socrates' metaphysical assumptions imply that such things are beautiful to the extent that they share in the nature of the Form of Beauty. Insofar as they point beyond themselves to a higher source of value, in whose nature they share, they have an instrumental value. The desiring agents of the Lower Mysteries do not appreciate sensible beautiful things as instances of this intelligible beauty. In failing to appreciate that fact they fail to pursue an object desired for its own sake alone.[27] An inferior experience of value is a limited creative environment which, in turn, hinders the production of a variety of excellences in the Lower Mysteries (212a). Their experience of beauty is limited to things that change over time, are beautiful to one person and not to another, and in one respect

---

[26] These two facts are related. It is because the philosopher, for example, wants to acquire knowledge about beauty that he pursues a particular kind of beauty in the way that he does – a beauty that exists always, forever in the same state, and perfectly.

[27] It is controversial whether one takes it that beautiful objects other than the Form are valuable only instrumentally, or whether they can be valued for their own sake (in as much as they embody the intrinsically valuable character of the Form) and instrumentally. If the latter then Socrates' argument would be weaker.

and not in others. If their creations are produced in such an environment, then their value, too, will reflect a beauty more perfectly realised elsewhere.

Although the desiring agents of the Lower Mysteries clearly want to secure something good, the rich variety of excellences they procure appears not to satisfy the criterion of being a final good in a further sense. Recall some examples. Some of these desiring agents produce children, whilst others produce a variety of excellences ranging from heroic deeds to poetry and lawmaking. The real end of all these excellences, though, resides not in the activities themselves (the producing of children, or poems, say), but in the possibility that such things will secure 'immortal memory', or honour, or fame for their producers (208c, d, 209d, e). In other words, such activities are not pursued for their own sake, but for the honour that results. Such excellences depend upon one's children turning out well, or books being well received, or shrines established in one's honour by the city. This is an insecure and unstable foundation upon which to build a flourishing life perhaps, depending as it does on the whims of others. And since their understanding of value is limited to things that change over time, are beautiful to one perceiver and not to another, and so on, there is nothing to ensure that their creations will be valued at all times, and to all perceivers, and so on.

Consider intellectual excellence, by contrast. This excellence is said to be genuine excellence 'because it is not an image that he is grasping, but the truth' (212a). Since such an excellence is genuine excellence, this will not, one supposes, fluctuate over time, appear excellent at one time and not at another, or in one respect and not in another, like the images produced by the desiring agents of the Lower Mysteries. This is a stable and secure good.[28] Intellectual excellence is also different because it is a possession of the mind, or soul, which is not dependent on any further event for its acquisition, such as one's children turning out well or, cults or shrines set up in one's honour. One does not think about the Form of Beauty in order to do something or other, or to be remembered by someone or other: 'There is the life', we are told, 'which a human being should live, in the contemplation of Beauty itself' (211d). We are asked to consider the activity of contemplating a supremely valuable object as an excellence, or perfection, of the human mind, or

---

[28] Compare Einstein's famous observation that 'Politics is for the present, while our equations are for eternity'.

soul, and, as such, as something of intrinsic value to its possessor. To the extent that we are persuaded that such an activity is desirable for its own sake, Socrates will also have persuaded us that contemplation is the sort of good that can satisfy our desire for happiness, and thereby that philosophy – the love of wisdom – is the best expression of desire.

Loving the Form and loving persons

The force of Socrates' argument seems to rely, in part, on the fact that the philosopher stands alone, as it were, at the top of the ascent, in need of no one else to secure his flourishing. This has suggested to some that Socrates has lost sight of the role of other persons in a flourishing life. This is puzzling if we expect, as many readers do, that this is a dialogue about interpersonal love. How could a discussion of interpersonal love be so spectacularly dehumanised by Socrates? On Socrates' view, are persons now relegated to being instances of a beauty more perfectly realised in the Form?[29] Part of the difficulty here arises when the term *eros* is construed as 'love', which seems to carry with it a strong association with persons. Reflecting on the substance of the speeches we can now appreciate better that what is under consideration in this work is the nature and aims of human desire more broadly, and the role that loving relationships might play in shaping those desires towards beneficial ends. Now, if we keep in mind that Socrates is discussing our desire, or aspiration, for happiness quite generally (205d), then his lack of focus on individual persons does not appear so stark. It is only the comic poet, after all, who finds the end of human fulfilment in the arms of another individual person. Seeing an individual as the source of all value and the centre of our happiness is, perhaps, a rather limited view to take of the rich possibilities for human happiness, and a heavy burden for any individual person to carry. Socrates, like many of his predecessors, is exploring a variety of good things on which our happiness can depend, such as honour or contemplation. In achieving the end that he advocates, individual persons are a source of wonder and reflection; for contemplation of Beauty is to be had by

---

[29] Gregory Vlastos famously argued that 'the cardinal flaw' in Plato's theory was that 'it does not provide for love of whole persons, but only for love of that abstract version of persons which consists of a complex of their best qualities'. He was referring to the fact that the philosopher uses beautiful bodies and souls 'like steps' to the contemplation of the source of all beauty: the Idea of beauty. See Vlastos (1981) 31.

reflecting broadly upon the nature of value, and the kinds of things that make bodies and souls into beautiful instances of their kind (210c). When we reflect upon the sorts of things that make decent souls into better souls, for example, we find that it is beautiful laws and practices that perform this role, and so we investigate them in turn. When we reflect on the feature that all fine bodies, souls and activities have in common, we are led to the source of their beauty. It is here that we can know and love the source of all beauty, and become productive of the highest kind of excellence.

But this is not the only role given to individual persons on his account. Placing the ascent within the larger context of the dialogue and its concerns suggests that Socrates has not lost sight of the nature and goals of interpersonal love relationships; rather, he is providing an account of the sorts of values that should inform such relationships. These are the context, if not the focus, of the entire account. As the other speeches amply demonstrated, it is on the basis of some conception of what is worth having or doing (however vague) that lovers advocate certain pursuits to their devotees. A praise of the beneficial effects of love involves showing the sorts of values that should inform such a relationship. This is part of the purpose of Socrates' argument for the superiority of the philosophical life. If loving relationships involve care and concern for others, and if the sort of pederastic relationships which concern the speakers in the dialogue were, at their best, educational relationships, then it is only when one has some sense of where human happiness resides that one can be a proper educator and muse to the young.[30] The end of Socrates' speech is the beginning, not the end, of a truly beneficial love relationship.[31]

Alcibiades' speech

If Socrates is making some such point, then a contemporary readership, familiar with the historical Socrates, may well have the following question for Plato. If the sort of love relationship advocated by Socrates

---

[30] The guide who leads the young person in the ascent to the Form can be seen as an example of a relationship informed by philosophical values.

[31] There is nonetheless a real difficulty in figuring out how the philosophical lover will integrate care and concern for others if contemplation of the form is where his happiness resides. Will his care for other persons mean that he is less happy? If so, what are the implications for Plato's ethics? Plato faced this issue again, though no less controversially, in the *Republic* where Socrates argues that, though happiness resides with the Forms, the philosopher should return to the cave of ordinary life for the business of ruling the ideal city.

is so beneficial, then why did Socrates fail with his own lovers? It is well known that Socrates was tried for corrupting the young (399 BC). His high profile relationship with the young Alcibiades, in particular, is typically held to have contributed to Socrates' downfall in the eyes of a populace still relatively fresh from its defeat by Sparta in the Peloponnesian War (404 BC). Alcibiades had persuaded the Athenians to embark on the disastrous Sicilian expedition (415 BC) with him as one of the generals, an event which contributed to their final defeat in the war. He was soon called back to Athens to face charges of impiety, charges of which he was cleared (407 BC). He was then given a command again, but was forced to withdraw to Thrace. By the end of this war Alcibiades had betrayed Athens to Sparta and Persia. The attempt to purge the city of its associations with such men and recover from the war forms the backdrop for Socrates' trial. If Alcibiades was an associate of Socrates, then perhaps Socrates was partly to blame for the corruption of this promising youth, at least. Plato was evidently not a man to hide from a challenge and he faces this one explicitly in the final speech of the dialogue.

Alcibiades enters the symposium, drunk, and escorted by flute girls. When he delivers his speech about Socrates and their relationship, we the readers, who have heard the account of love given by Socrates (as Alcibiades has not), are in a position to interpret the details in light of that account. Alcibiades' account reveals that although he desires the wisdom he perceives in Socrates, he believes it to be the sort of thing one can exchange for his physical charms (compare Agathon's behaviour at the start of the dialogue, 175c). When Socrates rejects his advances and advocates a relationship of joint inquiry, Alcibiades cannot stay the course.[32] There is a competing value pulling him away:

> What I have felt in the presence of this one man is what no one would think I had it in me to feel in front of anyone, namely shame. And it is only in front of him that I feel it, because I am well aware that I cannot argue against the conclusion that I should do as he says. Yet when I leave him I am equally aware that I am giving in to my desire for honour from the public, so I skulk out of his sight like a runaway slave. (216b)

---

[32] This can be seen as part of a broader theme in the dialogue whereby Socrates is concerned to revise not only the nature and goals of a love relationship, but how they are achieved.

This conflict between the attractions of wisdom and the sort of excellence that earns honour from the people is the very one argued out theoretically in Socrates' speech. Alcibiades' choice to organise his life around the pursuit of personal honour is one confirmed by post-Peloponnesian War rhetoric, and a reason given for the doomed Sicilian expedition. In this most dramatic of dialogues, Plato embodies the values advocated by the philosopher and others in the lives of particular men whose personal tragedies he calls to mind. In so doing he exonerates Socrates from any association with these terrible events. Socrates was not responsible for the corruption of this promising youth at least; the sorts of values perpetuated here by Agathon and his guests fostered this misguided love. The loss of this particular struggle between philosophy and the competing values of the city was to have a lasting effect on Athenian history.

Conclusion

The aim of this introduction has been to highlight some of the central arguments of the *Symposium*, and in so doing to show that this work relates in several ways to broader themes in the Platonic corpus. The *Symposium* belongs with those dialogues concerned with the moral education of the young, and its discussion of the nature and goals of loving relationships takes us to the heart of Plato's concern with the good life and how it is achieved. The fact that desires are seen to play such an important role in moral development draws on a theme elaborated in the *Republic*, and locates this text amongst many other ancient works concerned with the development of character and how that contributes to the good life. Though Plato leads us to the lofty heights of the Forms as the true end of our desire for good things and happiness, his account is nonetheless one that resonates beyond such abstractions. It is by prompting us to reflect more deeply on the relationship between our desires and their real end, and the role that our lovers might play in helping us to achieve it, that the *Symposium* really makes its mark.[33]

---

[33] I am grateful to Arif Ahmed and James Warren for comments on the Introduction, and in particular to Desmond Clarke, Hilary Gaskin, and Margaret Howatson for extensive written comments.

Chronology

BC

594	Constitutional reforms of Solon at Athens.
	Mid-sixth century, Athens ruled by a tyranny.
c.540	Heraclitus born at Ephesus.
533	First competition for the best tragedies held at Athens.
514	Hipparchus murdered by Harmodius and Aristogiton.
510	Hippias expelled from Athens.
508	Political reforms at Athens, leading to the foundation of democracy.
499	Ionia revolts unsuccessfully against Persian rule.
490	Persians invade Greece and are defeated at Marathon.
486	First competition for the best comedies held at Athens.
484	Aeschylus (b. 525) wins his first victory in the tragedy competitions.
480	Persians invade Greece for the second time, but after victory at Thermopylae suffer defeat at Salamis and Plataea. This date is taken as marking the beginning of the classical period of ancient Greece.
469	Socrates born.

468	Sophocles (b.c.496) wins his first victory in the tragedy competitions.
465	Euripides (b.c.485) first competes in the tragedy competitions.
461–429	Pericles, the Athenian democratic politician, most influential.
451	Alcibiades born.
450 (or earlier)	Aristophanes born.
445 (or a little earlier)	Agathon born.
431	Start of the Peloponnesian war between Sparta and Athens.
430	Plague at Athens.
429	Pericles dies of plague.
427 (or a little later)	Plato born.
424	Athens defeated at battle of Delium.
422	Spartan general Brasidas killed.
416	Agathon wins his first tragedy competition. The 'dramatic' date of the *Symposium*.
415	Athens decides to send an expedition to win control of Sicily, with Alcibiades as one of the generals. The profanation of the mysteries and the mutilation of the herms.
415–413	Sicilian expedition. Alcibiades is soon recalled to Athens but escapes into exile.
411	Democracy at Athens temporarily overthrown by oligarchic (aristocratic) revolutionaries known as 'the Four Hundred', but restored within a year.
404	Alcibiades assassinated. Athens surrenders to Sparta and is governed temporarily by the so-called Thirty Tyrants, oligarchs supported by Sparta.
403	Returning Athenian exiles help defeat the Thirty in battle. Democracy restored at Athens.
399	Trial and execution of Socrates.
387	Traditional date for the founding of the Academy at Athens, with Plato as head.

387–386	The Spartan dispersal of the city of Mantinea.
386	The (Persian) King's Peace.
384	Aristotle is born.
	The earliest plausible date for the writing of the *Symposium*.
347	Plato dies.
338	Defeat of Athens at the battle of Chaeronea and the loss of her independence to Philip of Macedon.
323	Death of Alexander the Great of Macedon, taken as marking the end of the classical period of ancient Greece.

Further reading

Background information on the institution of the Greek symposium and pederasty is available in several important essays in O. Murray, *Sympotika: A Symposium on the Symposium* (Oxford, 1990). Of particular interest for understanding pederastic relationships in Greek culture are J. M. Bremmer, 'Adolescents, *symposion*, pederasty', in the Murray collection. Also of interest here are K. J. Dover, *Greek Homosexuality* (London, 1978) and C. Calame, *The Poetics of Eros in Ancient Greece* (Princeton, 1999). For books on *eros* in Greek culture more broadly, interesting studies include P. W. Ludwig, *Eros and Polis* (Cambridge, 2002), and B. Thornton, *Eros: The Myth of Ancient Greek Sexuality* (Colorado, 1997).

For a discussion of the difficulties of Plato's use of the dialogue form and the possibilities of extracting Platonic doctrine from them, see M. Frede, 'Plato's arguments and the Dialogue Form' in Klagge and Smith (eds.) *Methods of Interpreting Plato and His Dialogues, Oxford Studies in Ancient Philosophy, Supplementary Volume* (Oxford, 1992), 201–19, and more recently, J. Beversluis, 'A Defence of Dogmatism in the Interpretation of Plato', *Oxford Studies in Ancient Philosophy*, volume XXXI (2006, Winter), 85–111.

Christopher Rowe's edition of Plato's *Symposium* (Aris and Phillips, 1998) provides a good commentary on the *Symposium*. For those with a reading knowledge of Greek, the edition of R.G. Bury is a treasure trove of insights (Cambridge, 1932). R. Hunter, *Plato's Symposium* (Oxford, 2004), offers an overview of the *Symposium* that is particularly sensitive to its literary and historical context. A more philosophical approach is taken by F. Sheffield, *Plato's Symposium: The Ethics of Desire* (Oxford, 2006).

For a discussion of some general themes in Plato's ethics, helpful books include A. W. Price, *Love and Friendship in Plato and Aristotle* (Oxford, 1989, with a new 1997 edition); T. Irwin, *Plato's Ethics* (Oxford, 1995); and J. Annas, *The Morality of Happiness* (Oxford, 1995) (which discusses ancient views of happiness, including Plato). The debate about whether Socrates' ethics in the *Symposium* is egoistic was started by G. Vlastos, 'The individual as an object of love' in Vlastos (ed.) *Platonic Studies* (Princeton, 1981), 1–34. A riposte is L.A. Kosman, 'Platonic Love', in W. H. Weikmeister, *Facets of Plato's Philosophy* (Assen, 1976), 53–69.

The following articles will be useful for a discussion of some of the specific issues raised in the introduction. An overview of Plato's theory of desire can be found in C. Kahn's 'Plato's Theory of Desire', *Review of Metaphysics* (1987) 41: 77–103. T. Penner's 'Thought and Desire in Plato' in Vlastos (ed.) *Plato, volume ii: Ethics, and Philosophy of Art and Religion; A Collection of Critical Essays* (New York, 1971), 96–119 focuses on the relationship between desire and belief in Plato, and A. Nehamas' 'Socratic Intellectualism' in A. Nehamas (ed.), *The Virtues of Authenticity* (Princeton, 1999), Chapter 2 reflects more broadly on Socratic intellectualism. Reflection on the method of the ascent to the Form of Beauty will benefit from R. Patterson, 'The Ascent passage in Plato's *Symposium*', *Proceedings of the Boston Area Colloquium in Ancient Philosophy* (1991) 7:193–214. For a collection of essays that explores some of the broader issues about knowledge in Plato and its relationship to Forms, see G. Fine, *Plato on Knowledge and Forms* (Oxford, 2003).

Translator's note

In this translation I have tried to write in modern standard English a version of Plato's *Symposium* that is faithful to the Greek, is not too tendentious, and is in tune with the current academic reception of the text. It is not a word-for-word translation (if such a thing were possible). There can be no close equivalence in readable English of the original words in the original order of clauses. Sentences in Plato can be very long, with complicated syntax. I have simplified the sentence structure and in a few cases rearranged the clauses for the sake of clarity and to make them follow a familiar English pattern.

Each speech in the *Symposium* has its individual style – grandiloquent, self-consciously exquisite, ironic, and so on, and each reflects on its speaker. Meaning itself can be inherent in style as well as in argument, and can change when individuality disappears in translation. Readers should be aware that a speech which seems vapid and repetitious to some readers of Plato's Greek may sound snappier in this translation. Conversely, much that is spare and witty in the original has, I regret to say, become ponderous. Compromises have to be made and there is a loss.

There is also difficulty in that the semantic range of a given Greek word does not necessarily correspond closely with that of its nearest English equivalent. For that reason any one Greek word may be translated variously in English, according to context. A glossary is included to give some help in fixing the meaning more exactly in particular instances.

Plato's text has not come down to us entirely as he wrote it; there are obvious, and some not so obvious, corruptions. In a few places where the Greek has long baffled many scholars the translation aims to give what appears to me to be the general sense, although not all Platonists will agree.

The text used is that of Kenneth Dover (Plato: *Symposium*, Cambridge University Press, 1980). The numbers and letters in the margin represent a system of reference now universally employed for the works of Plato. It dates back to the edition published by Stephanus in Geneva in the mid-sixteenth century.

I am very grateful indeed for the help and advice of several readers and in particular to Desmond Clarke, Roger Crisp, Frisbee Sheffield and Hilary Gaskin.

The Symposium ('The Drinking Party')

APOLLODORUS: I believe I am quite well prepared to relate the events 172a
you are asking me about, for just the other day I happened to be going
into Athens from my home in Phalerum[1] when an acquaintance of mine
caught sight of me from behind and called after me, jokily,[2]

'Phalerian! You there, Apollodorus! Wait for me, will you?'

So I stopped and waited.

'I have just been looking for you, Apollodorus. I wanted to get from
you the story about that party of Agathon's with Socrates, Alcibiades
and the rest, the time when they were all together at dinner, and to hear 172b
what they said in their speeches on the subject of love. Someone else
was telling me, who had heard about it from Phoenix, son of Philippus,
and he said that you knew about it too. Actually he could not give any
clear account of it, so you must tell me. You are in the best position to
report the words of your friend.[3] But tell me this first', he went on.
'Were you at that party yourself or not?'

'It certainly looks as if your informant was rather confused', I replied, 172c
'if you think the party you are asking about occurred recently enough
for me to be there'.

'Yes, I did think so', he replied.

Certain words in the text carry footnotes giving their (transliterated) Greek originals, or related
words, in italics. Explanations of these are to be found in the Glossary of Greek words. For all
names see the Glossary of names.
[1] Phalerum was the old harbour of Athens, roughly two miles south-west of the city.
[2] The point of the joke is not obvious.   [3] The friend is Socrates.

'But how could you think so, Glaucon?' I said. 'Don't you know that it is now many years[4] since Agathon lived in Athens, and it is not yet three years since I began to associate with Socrates and to make it my 173a daily business to know everything he says and does? Before that I used to think I was achieving something when I was in fact running round in circles aimlessly, in the most miserable state, just like you now, and I thought philosophy[5] was the last thing I should be doing'.

'Don't make fun of me', he said. 'Just tell me when that party took place'.

'When you and I were still boys', I replied, 'in the year when Agathon won the prize with his first tragedy[6] and on the day after he and the members of the cast held the sacrificial feast to celebrate the victory'.

'Oh, then it really was a long time ago', he replied. 'But who told you about it? Was it Socrates himself?'

173b 'Certainly not', I said. 'It was actually the man who told Phoenix, someone called Aristodemus of Cydathenaeum, a small man, who never wore any shoes. He had been at the party, and I think there was no more devoted admirer[7] of Socrates at that time. But of course I asked Socrates myself some questions afterwards about what I had heard from Aristodemus, and he confirmed what Aristodemus had said'.

'Then', said Glaucon, 'do tell me. The city road is in any case convenient for conversation between fellow-travellers'.

So it happened that as we went on our way we talked about the 173c speeches, with the result that, as I said at the beginning, I am quite well prepared. If you really want me to recount them to all of you as well, then that is what I had better do. Anyway, whenever I talk myself on any philosophical subject or I listen to others talking, quite apart from thinking it is doing me good I enjoy it enormously. But when I listen to other kinds of discussion, especially from people like you, rich money-makers, I get

---

[4] There is evidence to suggest that Agathon left Athens between 411 and 405 BC, and Socrates was put to death in 399 BC, so Plato is dating this purported encounter between Apollodorus and his friends to one of the last years of the fifth century BC.

[5] 'To do philosophy' translates *philosophein*.

[6] Ancient authority gives the date as the early spring of 416 BC. Plato too would have been a boy at the time.

[7] 'Admirer' is *erastēs*, the term for the (usually) older male partner in a homosexual relationship but it can also mean, as here, a devoted follower. Although the middle-aged Socrates followed the traditional Athenian pattern for homosexual love by at least professing to be in love with much younger men, it was widely observed that in reality it was the younger men who fell in love with him.

bored on my own account and at the same time I feel sorry for you, my companions, because you think you are achieving something when you are achieving nothing. On the other hand you perhaps believe that I am the one who is unfortunate,[8] and I suppose you are right. But in your case I don't merely suppose you are unfortunate, I *know* it.   173d

FRIEND: You are quite incorrigible, Apollodorus. You are always disparaging yourself and everyone else as well. I really do believe you think everyone except Socrates is miserable, starting with you. However you got that nickname, 'Softy',[9] I cannot imagine. You are always like this when you speak, raging against yourself and everyone else except Socrates.

APOLLODORUS: Obviously then, my dear friend, if I think as I do about myself and all of you I am completely mad!   173e

FRIEND: It is not worth quarrelling about these things now, Apollodorus. Please do what we asked you and tell us what they said in their speeches.

APOLLODORUS: Well then, those speeches went something like this – no, I shall begin at the beginning and try to tell you the whole story as Aristodemus told me.   174a

Aristodemus said that he and Socrates chanced to meet when the latter was fresh from the baths and wearing his sandals, two rare events for him, so he asked him where he was going, having got himself up so beautifully.

'To Agathon's for dinner', Socrates replied. 'I avoided the celebrations yesterday, being afraid of the crush, but I agreed I would come today. So that is why I have beautified myself like this, a beautiful guest for a beautiful host. But you, now: how do you feel about possibly coming to dinner when you have not been invited?'   174b

Aristodemus said that he replied, 'I shall do whatever you say'.

'Well, come with me then', said Socrates, 'and we will spoil the old saying by altering the words. We will make it say that "to *good* men's feasts[10] good men go unbidden". After all, Homer himself comes close not merely to spoiling it but to treating it with contempt. He represents Agamemnon as an exceptionally valiant warrior and Menelaus as "a

---

[8] *kakodaimon*; see *eudaimonein*.   [9] In Greek, *malakos*; some manuscripts read *manikos*, 'fanatic'.
[10] Agathon's name suggests the meaning 'good men'; see *agathos*. Socrates appears to have in mind a proverb which says, 'To *inferior* men's feasts good men go unbidden'.

faint-hearted spearman",[11] and when Agamemnon after sacrificing is
174c giving a banquet[12] he has Menelaus coming to the feast unbidden, and
so the worse man going to the feast of a better'.

Aristodemus said that, after listening to this, he replied, 'I am rather
afraid, Socrates, that in my case I shall come closer to Homer's version
than to yours, being an inferior man going uninvited to the feast of a
wise[13] one. If you take me along you had better see what excuse you will
give, because I shall not admit I came uninvited – I shall say I was
invited by you'.

174d ' "As we two go further on the way" ',[14] was the reply, 'we shall
decide on our story. Come on, now'.

After a conversation like this Aristodemus said they walked on. As
Socrates proceeded along the road he became absorbed in his own
thoughts and started to fall behind; when Aristodemus waited Socrates
174e told him to go on ahead. Arriving at Agathon's house Aristodemus
found the door open and himself standing there, he said, in a ridiculous
situation. One of the domestic servants immediately received him and
led him to where all the other guests had taken their places, and he
found them about to begin dinner. As soon as Agathon saw him he
called out, 'Aristodemus, how lucky! You are just in time for dinner. If
you have come for some other purpose, do postpone it. I was looking for
you yesterday to invite you but I could not find you. But how is it you
have not brought Socrates to join us?'

I turned round to look behind me, Aristodemus said, but I could not
see Socrates anywhere. So I replied that I had been invited there to
dinner by Socrates and that it was I in fact who had come with him.

'I am very glad you came', said Agathon, 'but where *is* the man?'
175a 'He was coming into the house behind me just now. I wonder myself
where he might be'.

'Go and look for Socrates and bring him in', said Agathon to a
servant. 'Now, Aristodemus, do take a place[15] beside Eryximachus'.

---

[11] *Iliad* 17. 588. [12] At *Iliad* 2. 408. [13] *sophos*.
[14] An altered quotation from Homer, *Iliad* 10. 224.
[15] At an Athenian dinner party and the subsequent drinking party (symposium), both of which
were attended only by men, the guests reclined on couches, one, two or three to a couch,
propping themselves on their left elbows and helping themselves to food and drink from small
tables in front of the couches. The couches were arranged in a rough rectangle in the dining
room. A servant would wash the guests' feet before they reclined. On the present occasion the

4

Aristodemus said that one servant brought him water to wash with before he took his place, while another appeared and said, 'Socrates is here but has withdrawn into your neighbours' doorway and is just standing there, and though I have been calling him he will not come inside'.

'How odd', said Agathon. 'Call him again and keep on calling him'.

'No', said Aristodemus, 'let him alone. This is one of his habits. 175b Sometimes he turns aside and stands still wherever he happens to be. He will come in very soon, I think. Don't disturb him, leave him alone'.

'Well, if you think so then that is what we had better do', replied Agathon. 'Now, you servants, lay your feast before the rest of us. At any rate you put on the table whatever you like when no one is supervising you – and supervising is something I have never yet done. So on this occasion treat these other guests, as well as me, as if you had invited us all to dinner yourselves. Look after us well and you will earn our thanks'. After this they started dinner, Aristodemus said, but still 175c Socrates did not come. Agathon kept trying to have him summoned but Aristodemus would not allow it. After delaying for a little while in that habitual way of his, Socrates eventually arrived, but by then they were about halfway through dinner. Agathon, who happened to be alone on the bottom couch, called out, 'Socrates, come over here beside me so that I may enjoy the benefit of being in contact with that piece of wisdom which came into your mind in that doorway. Obviously you are 175d now in possession of the answer you were looking for, otherwise you would not have stopped looking'.

Socrates sat down. 'It would be a happy state of affairs, Agathon, if wisdom were something that could flow between us through mere contact, from the one who is full to one who is empty, like water flowing along a strand of wool from a full cup to an empty one. If that is how it is with wisdom also, then I greatly value having the place next to you because I think that I shall get my fill from you of your abundant and 175e beautiful wisdom. My own wisdom is certainly of an inferior sort, and, like a dream, of doubtful reality, whereas yours is already brilliant and full of promise – witness the fact that it was so conspicuous the day before yesterday and shone forth from you so splendidly, young as you are, in the presence of more than thirty thousand Greek spectators'.

bottom couch, probably furthest from the door, was occupied by the host Agathon (175c). Phaedrus occupied the first couch (177d).

'Socrates, you are being sarcastic',[16] said Agathon. 'A little later on you and I will each plead our claim to wisdom, and Dionysus[17] will be our judge. But now you must pay attention to your dinner before anything else'.

176a   After this, said Aristodemus, Socrates arranged himself on the couch and ate his dinner along with all the rest, and when they had poured libations and sung in praise of the god and done all the customary things, they turned to the question of drinking. According to Aristodemus, Pausanias was the first to speak, roughly as follows.

'Well now, gentlemen', he said, 'how shall we make our drinking easy for ourselves? I must say to you that after yesterday's bout I am really in very poor shape and I could do with a breathing space. I imagine that is 176b the case with most of you who were at yesterday's celebrations, so think about how we might make our drinking as easy as possible'.

'This is a very good idea of yours, Pausanias', Aristophanes replied, 'making it a first requirement to give ourselves some respite from drinking. I speak as one of those soaked in drink yesterday'.

Eryximachus, the son of Acumenus, had been listening. 'Very well said', he added. 'But there is still one of you I should like to hear from as to whether he feels strong enough to drink – Agathon?'

'No', said Agathon, 'I am certainly not up to it either'.

176c   'It would be a stroke of luck for us, I think', continued Eryximachus, 'that is, for Aristodemus, Phaedrus, and me, and for our other friends here, if you, the most stalwart drinkers, have now given up. We always did have weak heads. I am not counting Socrates; he is unaffected either way, so he will not mind whichever we do. So, since it seems to me that no one here present is keen on drinking much wine, perhaps I would not be too unpopular if I spoke the truth about the nature of drunk- 176d enness. What has become very clear to me as a result of my profession as a doctor is that drunkenness is bad for people, and I would not care to drink a lot myself if I could avoid it, or recommend doing so to anyone else, especially if that person had a hangover from the previous day'.

According to Aristodemus, Phaedrus of Myrrhinous joined in. 'I for one always take your advice, especially in medical matters, and on this 176e occasion the rest will do so too if they are sensible'. At this they all

---

[16] *hubristes*; see *hubrizein* and footnote 206.

[17] Dionysus is the patron-god of the theatre, where Agathon won his victory. He is also the god who introduced wine to humans, which Agathon expects they will soon be drinking at the symposium which will follow dinner. A 'contest in wisdom' could be considered to take place at 199c–201c.

agreed not to make heavy drinking the rule for the present party, but to drink only as much as they would enjoy.

'Well then', said Eryximachus, 'since it is settled that each of us should drink just so much as he wants, and there is no compulsion, I have another suggestion to make about the girl who plays the *aulos*[18] who has just come in: let us tell her to go away and play to herself or, if she likes, to the women in their rooms, while for this evening we entertain each other with talk. And if you like I am ready with a proposal about the kind of talk we might have'.

They all welcomed his suggestion and asked him to explain further. So he did. 'For what I am going to say, I will begin in the manner of Euripides' Melanippe:[19] "not mine is the story". My suggestion comes from Phaedrus here. He is always complaining to me. "Isn't it shocking, Eryximachus", he says, "that while some other gods have had hymns and paeans composed for them by the poets, not a single one of all the many poets that have ever been has composed an encomium to the god Love, despite his great antiquity and importance! Just consider for a moment those good[20] sophists[21] such as the excellent Prodicus: they write prose eulogies of heroes[22] like Heracles, which is perhaps not very surprising, but I once came across a book by a learned man in which salt was the subject of extraordinary praise because of its usefulness – and you might find quite a few other things similarly eulogised. To think that people devote so much effort to subjects like that, but no one to this day has undertaken to celebrate Love in the way he deserves! So completely has this great god been neglected".

'It seems to me that Phaedrus has a point. I should therefore very much like[23] to gratify him in this matter and make a contribution, and I think also that this is a fitting occasion for those of us here present to pay honour to the god. If you too think as I do, we would have plenty to occupy us if we passed the time in making speeches. My proposal is that each of us should make a speech in praise of Love,[24] the finest he can manage, going from left

177a

177b

177c

177d

---

[18] A reeded pipe; normally a pair of *auloi* was played. Professional players and other entertainers were hired for parties.

[19] The tragedy *Melanippe the Wise*, by Euripides, does not survive, but the line partly cited above ends: 'I heard it from my mother'.

[20] *chrestos.*   [21] *sophistes.*   [22] See Glossary of names under **Heroes**.   [23] *epithumein.*

[24] Eryximachus, following Phaedrus's lead, apparently intends the subject of the speeches to be Eros, the male god of Love (who was not as celebrated at this time nor as strongly characterised as Aphrodite, goddess of Love). However, in many of the speeches that follow, the subject

to right, and, since Phaedrus is occupying the first place on the left and is also the originator of the subject, he should begin'.

'No one will vote against you, Eryximachus', said Socrates. 'I would hardly say no, since the only subject I can claim to know about is love,[25] and the same is true I rather think of Agathon and Pausanias,[26] and certainly true of Aristophanes, whose whole time is taken up with Dionysus and Aphrodite.[27] In fact it is true of everyone I see here. However, I should say that the arrangement is hardly fair on those of us who will be speaking last; but if those before us don't disappoint, and speak well, we shan't complain. Let Phaedrus go first and speak in praise of Love, and good luck to him'.

All the rest echoed his sentiments and repeated Socrates' instruction to begin. Now, Aristodemus did not entirely remember all that each speaker said, nor do I[28] remember everything that Aristodemus told me, but I will tell you what seemed to me particularly worth recording from the most memorable speeches.

Aristodemus told me, as I have said, that Phaedrus was the first to speak, and he began with the point that Love is a great god and particularly revered by men and gods by reason of his birth.[29] 'It is because he is the oldest of the gods that he is honoured', he said, 'and there is good evidence for this. Love has no parents, and none have ever been ascribed to him by anyone, prose-writer or poet. The poet Hesiod says[30] that first of all Chaos came into being,

"then there was
broad-bosomed Earth, the eternally firm foundation of all things,
and Love".

fluctuates between the god and the emotion of love, and in some places the word 'love' even seems to stand for the lover. This would have caused the Greeks fewer problems than it may cause readers of this translation, because the former did not distinguish in writing between upper- and lower-case letters. Most current texts and translations attempt to distinguish between Love and love, but the reader should be aware that in any translation the choice of upper- or lower-case initials is inevitably somewhat arbitrary.

[25] 'The subject of love' translates [*ta*] *erotica*; see glossary.
[26] Well known to be lovers; see 193b.
[27] In the view attributed here to Socrates, Aristophanes' comedies are all concerned with drink and sex, the respective provinces of those gods. Dionysus is also the patron-god of the theatre; see Glossary of names.
[28] Apollodorus, the narrator of the dialogue.   [29] *genesis*.
[30] *Theogony*, 116–17 and 120. It was the early Greek poets, especially Hesiod, who preserved the stories about the mythical past.

'Acusilaus too agrees with Hesiod and says that after Chaos there came into being these two, Earth and Love. And Parmenides also says of the origin[31] of Love,

> "First of all gods was fashioned Love".

'So it is widely agreed that Love is the oldest of the gods, and he is also the source of our greatest blessings.[32] For I certainly cannot say what greater blessing there can be for any man to have right from youth than a virtuous[33] lover,[34] or what can be better for a lover than a beloved boy[35] who is himself virtuous. For those feelings which ought to be the lifelong guide of men whose aim is to live a good[36] life cannot be implanted either by advantageous connexions or public honours or wealth or anything else so well as they are by love. And what are those feelings? Shame[37] at dishonourable[38] and pride[39] in honourable behaviour. Without these feelings it is not possible either for a state or for an individual to do any noble or great work. Therefore I declare that if any man who is in love were to be revealed doing something dishonourable or submitting dishonourably to someone without defending himself, because of cowardice, he would not find it as painful to be seen by his father or his friends or anyone like that as he would to be seen by his beloved. Clearly the same is true in the case of the beloved, that he feels particularly ashamed if ever he is seen by his lovers to be involved in something dishonourable. If only some means might be found for a state or an army to consist of pairs of lovers, there would be no better people to run their country, for they would avoid any act that brought disgrace and would compete with each other in winning honour. Moreover they would be victorious over virtually every other army, even if they were only few in number, as long as they fought side by side. Certainly a man in love who deserted his post or threw away his arms would mind less being seen by the whole world than by his beloved; sooner than this he would choose to die a thousand deaths. And as for abandoning his beloved or failing to go to his aid in danger – no one is so cowardly that he cannot be inspired to courage[40] by Love himself, to be the equal of the man who is very courageous[41] by nature. It is exactly as Homer describes a god

178c

178d

178e

179a

179b

---

[31] *genesis.*   [32] *agathos.*   [33] *chrestos.*   [34] *erastes.*

[35] *eromenos*, one of two terms (the other is *paidika*) for the younger male in a pederastic relationship. See Introduction p.viii.

[36] *kalos.*   [37] *aischune.*   [38] *aischros.*   [39] *philotimia.*   [40] *arete.*   [41] *aristos*; see *agathos.*

'breathing might' into some of the heroes:[42] in just the same way Love provides from his own being this inspiration for those in love.

'There is another point. Only those in love[43] are prepared to die for one another, women as well as men. Every Greek will find sufficient evidence for this claim in the example of Alcestis, the daughter of Pelias. She was the only person willing to die for her husband even 179c though he had a father and a mother still living. She so much surpassed them in devotion[44] because of her love[45] that she made them look like strangers to their own son, related to him only in name. When she had actually given up her life for him, so noble did it seem not only to men but also to the gods, that they sent back her soul[46] from the Under-world. Out of the many that have done great deeds, she is one of very few who have been granted this privilege; yet the gods sent back her 179d soul because of their great admiration for what she did. So they too pay particular honour to the zeal and courage[47] that come from love. In the case of Orpheus, however, the son of Oeagrus, they sent him back from the Underworld without achieving his object: they showed him only a phantom of the wife he had come to recover, and did not give her back to him in the flesh, because they thought he lacked spirit; he was only a lyre-player and did not dare actually to die, as Alcestis did, for the sake of love. Instead he contrived to enter the Underworld while he was still alive. So, because of this they punished him, and brought about his death at the hands of women.

179e 'Achilles, the son of Thetis, however, they honoured and sent to the Isles of the Blest.[48] For when he found out from his mother that if he killed Hector he too would die, but if he did not kill him he would return home and live to old age, he nevertheless dared to make the choice of standing up for his lover Patroclus[49] and avenging him; thus 180a he also died, and died for his sake. (Aeschylus actually talks nonsense when he asserts that it was Achilles who was the lover of Patroclus: Achilles was not only more beautiful than Patroclus but also more

---

[42] As Apollo into Aeneas at *Iliad* 20.110. [43] 'those in love', in Greek *hoi erontes*; see *eran*.
[44] *philia*; see *philein*. [45] *eros*. [46] *psuche*. [47] *arete*.
[48] In Greek myth, islands in the legendary far west of the Greek world where after death specially favoured mortals, notably some of the heroes, pass a blissful afterlife, rather than having a phantom existence in the Underworld like everyone else.
[49] Homer in the *Iliad* did not make Achilles and Patroclus lovers, but Aeschylus represents them as such in *Myrmidons*, a lost tragedy from which a few quotations survive.

beautiful than all the rest of the heroes, and still beardless; and according to Homer he was much younger.[50]) As a consequence the gods, out of extreme admiration, honoured Achilles to an exceptional degree for having such a high regard for his lover. Although the gods show particular honour to the kind of excellence that comes from passionate love, it is those cases where the beloved shows his devotion[51] to his lover rather than the other way round that they appreciate and admire more and reward more generously, because a lover has a god within him and he is thus more akin to the divine than the beloved. This is why the gods paid more honour to Achilles than to Alcestis and sent him to the Isles of the Blest.

180b

'These are my reasons, then, for saying that Love is the oldest of gods and most worthy of honour, and most powerful in helping men achieve excellence and happiness[52] both during life and after death'.

This was, roughly speaking, the speech Phaedrus made, according to Aristodemus, and after him there were some other speeches which Aristodemus did not altogether remember. Passing over these he related next the speech of Pausanias.

180c

'It seems to me, Phaedrus, that our subject has not been set out in the right way', said Pausanias. 'I mean that we have simply been told to deliver an encomium on Love, just like that. If there were only one Love it would be all very well, but in fact that is not the case: Love is not single, and that being so it is better to state first of all which sort of Love should be praised. I shall therefore try to put this right by first explaining which Love is the one to be praised, and then by praising the god in the way he deserves.

180d

'We all know that Aphrodite is always accompanied by Love. If there were only a single Aphrodite there would only be a single Love. But since there are two Aphrodites there must be two Loves also. And it cannot be denied that there are two goddesses. One, older obviously, is the daughter of Uranus and had no mother, and we call her "Heavenly[53]

---

[50] See *Iliad* 11.786–7.
[51] *agapan.* The general Greek assumption was that in a pederastic relationship only the lover felt sexual desire, *eros*, and the beloved reciprocated with affection and admiration. It appears from 179c (see footnote 45) that Phaedrus thought Alcestis was motivated by sexual love and so not strictly comparable with a beloved boy.
[52] *eudaimonia.*
[53] In Greek, *Ouranios*, 'Uranian', i.e. related to Ouranos, 'Heaven', the god whose name is commonly spelled Uranus in English. The Greeks had two stories about the birth of Aphrodite.

Aphrodite"; the younger is the child of Zeus and Dione and we call her
180e "Common[54] Aphrodite". It follows then that the Love who works with
the latter Aphrodite should correctly be called "Common Love" and
the other "Heavenly Love".

'All the gods deserve our praise, but however that may be, what I have
to do now is describe the sphere of activity that is the concern of each of
the two Loves. To begin with, it is true of every activity that it is in itself
181a neither right nor wrong.[55] Take what we are doing now, drinking or
singing or talking. None of these activities is right in itself; the manner of
its doing decides how it will turn out. Only if it is done in the right and
proper way is it right; if not, it is wrong. Now, the same is true of loving
and of Love: not every Love is right and deserves our praise,[56] only the
Love who directs us to love in the right way.

'The Love who belongs to Common Aphrodite is truly common and
181b engages in his activity as opportunity offers. This is the Love that inferior
people experience. In the first place men of this sort love women quite as
much as boys,[57] and secondly, their bodies more than their souls, and
thirdly, the stupidest people possible, since they have regard only for the
act itself and do not care whether it is rightly done or not. Hence their
activity is governed by chance, and as likely to be bad as good. The reason
is that the Common Aphrodite, with whom this Love is associated, is far
younger than the other Aphrodite, and because of her parentage she has
181c characteristics both of the male and of the female.

'However, the Love who accompanies the heavenly goddess (and
who does not descend from the female but only from the male) is the
love of boys, and that goddess is older and entirely free from wantonness.[58] Hence those who are inspired by this love incline to the male,

One said that she was the daughter of Zeus and Dione (compare 203b and footnote 156), the
other that she belonged to the previous generation of gods and rose fully formed out of the sea
near Cyprus from the foam surrounding the severed genitals of Uranus (grandfather of Zeus).

[54] In Greek, *Pandemos*, 'belonging to all the people'; hence, 'popular', 'common' and so 'ordinary',
'vulgar'.

[55] *kalos* and *aischros*. Throughout Pausanias' speech, 'right' and 'wrong' translate respectively the
Greek *kalos* and *aischros* (in their various forms; see glossary). Those who argue that these
concepts are not found among the Greeks have a strong case. Nevertheless, I have chosen to use
'right' and 'wrong' here because the tone of this particular speech suggested to me that these are
the nearest equivalent in English to the speaker's meaning. Those who do not agree might
prefer to substitute 'noble' and 'disgraceful' as appropriate.

[56] It looks as if the statement at 180e, that 'all gods deserve our praise', was merely a conventional
phrase to ward off possible retribution from the gods.

[57] *paides*, plural of *pais*.   [58] *hubris*.

preferring what has by nature more vigour and intelligence. Moreover, even among men who love younger members of their own sex it is possible to recognise those who are motivated purely by this heavenly love, in that they do not love boys before the stage when their intelli- 181d gence begins to develop, which is near the time when they begin to grow a beard. I believe that those who wait until then to embark on a love affair are prepared to spend their whole life with this individual and to live in partnership with him. They will not take him at a time when he is young and inexperienced, and then deceive him, contemptuously leaving him and running off to someone else.

'There ought really to be a law against starting a love affair with mere boys, to prevent a great deal of effort being spent on something of uncertain outcome, because with young boys it is uncertain how well or badly in body or soul[59] they will turn out. Good men of course lay down 181e this rule for themselves of their own accord, but some similar restriction should be imposed on those lovers of the common sort, just as we prevent them as far as we can from having love affairs with free-born women.[60] It is men like these who have given rise to disapproval and caused some 182a people to go so far as to state that gratifying[61] lovers is wrong, but their disapproval is based on the ill-judged and improper behaviour of this latter kind of lovers, since certainly no activity that is carried on in a decent and lawful manner can justly be called blameworthy.

'Now, in many states their conventional attitude to love has been defined in straightforward terms and is consequently easy to understand, but the attitude here in Athens, and also in Sparta,[62] is complex. In Elis and Boeotia[63] and wherever men are not skilled in argument, 182b they simply have a rule that it is fine to gratify lovers, and no one young or old would say that it was wrong. The reason is, I suppose, that, not being good speakers, they want to spare themselves the trouble of trying

---

[59] *psuche.*

[60] In Athens, as in ancient Greece in general, women who were not slaves were under the guardianship of their father, husband or nearest male relation, who exercised tight legal control of their sexual activity.

[61] In Plato's Greek a youth is euphemistically said to 'gratify' (*charizesthai*) his lover when he grants him sexual favours.

[62] The phrase 'in Sparta' is in all the manuscripts but several editors prefer to delete it as being inappropriate, or to put it after 'Elis', where they think it more appropriate (one reason being that Spartans were notoriously 'not skilled in argument').

[63] Independent states in Greece.

to win over young men with persuasive speech. However, in much of Ionia and elsewhere, and in the Persian empire generally, the conventional view is that gratifying lovers is wrong.[64] The Persians condemn it, as they also condemn philosophy and going to gymnasia,[65] because

182c their form of government is tyranny.[66] I imagine it does not suit the rulers that high aspirations or ties of friendship and loyalty should arise among their subjects, and these are the emotions which are likely to be produced by love more than by anything else. This is the painful lesson which our tyrants here in Athens learned, since it was the love of Aristogiton for Harmodius and the latter's unwavering devotion in return that put an end to their rule.[67] Thus in places where it has been

182d established as wrong to gratify lovers, this attitude exists because of the moral failings of those who established it: ruthless self-interest in the rulers, and cowardice in the ruled. But where the practice is simply thought to be fine, this attitude exists because of the laziness of mind[68] of those who established it.

'Compared with this our laws and customs here in Athens have been laid down to much better effect, but as I was saying they are not easy to understand. Think about it. It is said to be finer to conduct a love affair openly rather than secretly, and especially with the noblest and best individuals, even if they are less good-looking than some. Again, it is said that the degree of encouragement given by everyone to the lover is astonishing, which does not suggest he is about to do something dis-

182e graceful. If he succeeds in his aim people think it is to his credit; only if he fails is it a disgrace. When the lover in his attempt to win his beloved performs extraordinary acts our custom deems his actions praiseworthy, though if anyone else were to dare to behave in this way in the pursuit of any other aim and with anything other than this in view, he would

183a incur the strongest disapproval.

---

[64] Plato is writing here of his own time (in the decade after 385; see footnote 109), when the Greeks living in Ionia on the west coast of Asia Minor came under Persian rule after 386 BC.

[65] Gymnasia, being places of education as well as of nude physical exercise, offered pederastic and homosexual opportunities.

[66] The name given to the rule of an absolute monarch, and usually of one who had seized power illegally. The Persians at this period were ruled by a dynastic monarchy. After the rise of democracy in Athens during the fifth century BC the idea of tyranny became repugnant to the Athenians.

[67] Harmodius and Aristogiton killed Hipparchus, brother of the Athenian tyrant Hippias, in 514 BC.

[68] *psuche*.

'If a man wanted to get money from someone, for example, or gain a political office or some other position of power, just imagine him being willing to do the kind of things that lovers do to woo their beloved: begging him with supplications and entreaties, swearing oaths, sleeping in his doorway, willingly enduring the kind of slavery even a slave would not put up with. Friends and enemies alike would prevent him from acting in this way, his enemies jeering at his obsequiousness and servility, his friends remonstrating with him and feeling embarrassed by his actions. But when it is a lover doing all these things people find his behaviour quite charming, and our custom allows him to act as he does without reproach, the assumption being that he is engaged in some splendid enterprise. The strangest thing of all is that when a lover swears an oath and breaks it – at least this is what people say – he and he alone is forgiven by the gods, for an oath sworn in passion, they say, has no validity. 183b

'So, as the convention here in Athens has it, a lover is granted complete licence by both gods and men. Accordingly one might suppose that, in this city, being in love or showing affection towards a lover are regarded as splendid for both parties. 183c

'On the other hand, consider how fathers put tutors in charge of their sons when the latter have attracted lovers, and instruct them not to let the sons speak to their lovers. Consider also how the boys' peers and friends jeer at them if they see anything of the sort going on, and their elders do nothing to prevent or rebuke the jeering as they would if what was being said was out of order. Anyone seeing all this would surely conclude that, contrary to what he thought before, behaviour of this kind is regarded here as very wrong indeed. But the truth is, I think, as I said at the start, that it is not a simple matter. The practice is neither right in itself nor wrong in itself, but it is right if it is done in the right way and wrong if it is done in the wrong way. It is wrongly done to gratify a bad man, or gratify in a bad way, and it is rightly done to gratify a good[69] man, or gratify in the right way. 183d

'The bad man is the lover of the common sort, the one who loves the body rather than the soul. He is not constant, because the thing he loves is not constant. As soon as the physical bloom that he fell in love with begins to fade, "he flits away and is gone",[70] revealing the worthlessness 183e

[69] *chrestos.* [70] A reference to Homer, *Iliad* 2.71.

of his protestations and promises. But the lover who loves a virtuous character remains constant for life, because he is joined with that which remains constant.

184a   'Now, our custom here in Athens aims to put both classes of lovers well and truly to the test, the good to be gratified, the bad shunned. Accordingly the lover is encouraged to pursue but the beloved to run away, because then a competition or test is set up which will reveal to which of the two classes the lover and the beloved respectively belong. This is the reason why, in the first place, we consider it shameful for the beloved to be won over by a lover too quickly: time should elapse, for after all, time seems to be a good test of most things. Secondly, we also consider it shameful for him to be won over by money or political

184b   influence, and this is the case both if he is subjected to threats and submits without resisting, and if he is treated kindly with financial or political inducements and fails to reject these with contempt. For neither situation seems to offer lasting security, quite apart from the fact that no true friendship can develop on that basis.

    'So, according to our custom only one method is left by which the beloved can gratify his lover in the right way. I have already explained how here in Athens we accept it as customary for lovers willingly to

184c   endure any form of slavery for the sake of a beloved without being reproached for obsequiousness. There is one other form of voluntary slavery – but only one – which we also accept and which is beyond reproach. This is the slavery that is directed to excellence. We take the view that if someone is willing to devote himself to another person in the belief that through that person he will become a better man himself in some kind of wisdom[71] or in any other part whatever of excellence,[72] then this kind of voluntary slavery is not wrong, nor is it obsequiousness. It is necessary therefore that these two customs – the one to do with loving boys, the other with pursuing wisdom[73] and the other parts

184d   of excellence – should exist each in the appropriate partner if it is going to turn out to be right for the beloved to gratify the lover. For then, when a lover and his beloved come together, each will have his own

---

[71] *sophia.*

[72] As well as wisdom (*sophia*, which in this context means skills or accomplishments), the other parts of a man's virtue or personal excellence (*arete*) are justice, good sense or self-control (*sophrosune*) and bravery, together with piety.

[73] 'pursuing wisdom' here translates *philosophia.*

principle.[74] The lover will believe that by being of service in any way to the beloved who has gratified him he will be justified in so serving him. The beloved will believe that by helping in any way the one who is making him wise and good he too will be justified in so helping him. Thus the lover will be able to contribute to his beloved's understanding[75] and excellence in general, and the beloved will seek to acquire 184e these qualities for his education and his wisdom in general. Therefore, when these two principles exist and are directed to the same end, then and only then does it come about that it is right for a beloved to gratify his lover; otherwise, not.

'In this circumstance, even being deceived is not shameful, but in all other cases gratification brings shame on the beloved whether he is deceived or not. For if the beloved, believing his lover to be rich, gratifies him for the sake of money, but is deceived and gets no money 185a because the lover turns out to be poor, it is still shameful because a beloved like that seems to reveal his true character. He shows that he is prepared to do any service to anyone for the sake of money, and this behaviour is not right. By the same token, if a beloved gratifies a lover on the grounds that the man is good and that he himself will become a better person through that man's love, but is deceived and the man turns out to be bad and devoid of excellence, in this case his being deceived is a noble error. This beloved too seems to have made clear his 185b own character, but *he* shows that he is keen to do anything for anybody for the sake of excellence and becoming a better person, and this is the noblest thing of all. Thus it is entirely right to gratify a lover when it is for the sake of excellence. This is the love that belongs to the heavenly goddess, and it is itself heavenly and of great value to the state and to individuals alike, since it compels the lover to take great care with regard to his own excellence and the beloved to do the same. But all 185c other kinds of love belong to the other goddess, the common one.

'This is my contribution, Phaedrus, the best I can deliver on the spur of the moment, on the subject of Love'.

Pausanias came to a pause[76] (those experts in rhetoric[77] teach me to speak in this balanced way). Aristodemus said that it was Aristophanes'

---

[74] *nomos.* [75] *phronesis.*

[76] 'Pausanias came to a pause' translates the Greek *Pausaniou pausamenou*, two very similar-sounding words, each with four syllables of corresponding length; hence the reference to balance.

[77] 'the *sophoi*' (plural of *sophos*; see *sophia*).

turn to speak, but either through over-eating or for some other reason he 185d had an attack of hiccups and could not do so. The doctor Eryximachus was reclining on the next couch, so Aristophanes turned to him. 'You are just the person, Eryximachus,[78] either to put a stop to my hiccups or to speak instead of me until I stop myself'.

'I will do both', replied Eryximachus. 'I will speak in your place, and you can speak in mine when you have recovered. If in the course of my speech you hold your breath for a while and your hiccups are disposed 185e to stop, all well and good. But if that fails, gargle with water. However, if the hiccups are very persistent, find something to tickle your nose with and make yourself sneeze. If you do this once or twice even the most obstinate case will stop'.

'Start speaking now', said Aristophanes, 'and I shall do what you say'. So Eryximachus began to address them.

'Well now, Pausanias made a good start to his speech but failed 186a to end it adequately, so I think that I have to try to give it a proper conclusion. It seems to me that Pausanias is right in distinguishing two kinds of Love; but the fact is that Love influences not only human souls[79] in response to physical beauty,[80] he has influence on all other things and on their responses as well. Love pervades the bodies of all animals and all that is produced in the earth, which means that Love pervades virtually everything that exists. All this is something I feel I 186b have observed from my own profession of medicine, and I know how great and wonderful the god is and how his influence extends over all things both human and divine.

'I shall start by speaking about medicine, in order to give pride of place to that profession.[81] It is the nature of bodies to have these two kinds of Love in them. As everyone agrees, bodily health and bodily sickness are different and unlike things, and when things are unlike the objects of their love and desire are unlike also. So love in the healthy body is one thing, and love in the unhealthy body is quite another. Now, Pausanias was saying a moment ago that it is right to gratify good men and wrong to 186c gratify the immoral, and so it is with the body. It is right and, indeed, obligatory to gratify the good and healthy parts; that is what we call medicine. It is wrong to gratify the bad and diseased parts, and one

---

[78] His name could be punned upon as 'Hiccup-fighter'.   [79] *psuche.*
[80] The Greek indicates male beauty, but could include female beauty.   [81] *techne.*

truly versed in the practice of medicine will refuse to do so. In brief, medicine is knowledge of the influence of love on the body in respect of repletion and depletion;[82] and the man with the best medical knowledge is the one who can distinguish the right from the wrong kind of love in these processes. And the man who knows how to bring about change so as to convert the one into the other, and who also knows how to implant love where it is required and remove it where it is not, is a skilful practitioner.[83] In fact he must be able to reconcile the most hostile elements in the body and make them love[84] one another. The most hostile are the extreme opposites, hot and cold, bitter and sweet, dry and moist, and so on. It was because he knew how to impart love and unanimity to these opposites that our forebear Asclepius founded our profession,[85] or so say the poets – like those here[86] – and I believe them. Medicine therefore is, as I say, entirely directed by this god, as are gymnastic training and agriculture also.

    Now, it is obvious to anyone who gives even the slightest thought to the matter that the same reconciliation of opposites applies in music. This perhaps is what Heraclitus meant,[87] although his actual wording is not accurate; for he says of "the One"[88] that "it is in agreement while being in disagreement with itself, like the harmony[89] of the taut bow or the lyre". However, to speak of a harmony as being in disagreement with itself, or as existing when it is composed of elements still in disagreement, is quite absurd. But perhaps what he meant was that harmony is created out of elements, namely the high and the low, that were originally in disagreement but were subsequently brought into agreement through the art of music. For of course harmony could not arise out of the elements high and low while they were still in disagreement, because harmony is concord and concord is a kind of agreement, and agreement is impossible between elements that are in disagreement as long as they remain

186d

186e

187a

187b

---

[82] Ill-health was sometimes ascribed to an imbalance of elements in the body, which might be thought to be overfull of one element and empty of another.

[83] *agathos demiourgos.*   [84] *eran.*   [85] *techne.*   [86] Agathon and Aristophanes.

[87] The philosopher Heraclitus was notorious for the obscurity of his sayings. This saying can be found in H. Diels and W. Kranz, *Die Fragmente der Vorsokratiker* (often reprinted), Vol. 1, *Herakleitos* B51.

[88] The universe.

[89] *harmonia*; the fundamental meaning is 'a fitting together', 'structure', but the word has musical connotations also. 'Harmony' as understood in ancient Greek music does not exactly correspond with the modern notion of harmony.

in that state. It is impossible to create harmony where instead of agreement there is disagreement. The same is true of rhythm. Rhythm is created when elements which were originally in disagreement, namely

187c the fast and the slow, are subsequently brought into agreement. Here it is music that creates agreement in all these things by implanting mutual love and unanimity between the different elements, just as in the previous case it was medicine. Music too, therefore, is knowledge of the influence of love, in this case in respect of harmony and rhythm.

'Now, in the construction of harmony and rhythm there is no difficulty in discerning the influence of love, and love as a duality is not as

187d yet in evidence here. But when it is a case of employing rhythm and harmony in real life, either when creating new music, that is to say in composition, or when making correct use of tunes and metres that already exist, that is to say in education,[90] at this point difficulties arise and there is need of a skilful practitioner. We return yet again to the same theme, that it is the well-ordered[91] individuals, including those who, while not yet well-ordered, will be helped by love to become so, who should be gratified, and their love safeguarded. Theirs is the beautiful, the heavenly Love, the Love that comes from the muse

187e Urania.[92] But the other Love, the common one, comes from Polymnia, and should be used, if at all, with caution, so that the pleasure he brings may be enjoyed but no licentiousness implanted. Similarly, in my own profession, it is no small effort to deal properly with the appetites stimulated by cookery in order that the pleasure this brings may be enjoyed without ill effect. So, in music, in medicine and in every thing else, human as well as divine, one must, so far as possible, watch out for

188a both kinds of Love; for they are both present.

'Even the seasons of the year have a full measure of both kinds of Love in their composition. When the elements I was mentioning just now, hot and cold, dry and wet, enjoy the advantage of orderly love in

---

[90] This refers to that part of elementary education which consisted of learning poetry by heart and then how to sing it to the lyre.

[91] *kosmioi*; see *kosmos*.

[92] 'The heavenly one', the name of one of the Muses, who were the goddesses of artistic inspiration. Eryximachus is suggesting that the poetry and music inspired by Urania is morally good, but the kind inspired by Polymnia (another Muse; her name may also be spelled Polumnia) might not be so. The name Polymnia, 'she of many hymns', suggests plurality and so, perhaps, vulgarity. The *Republic* suggests that Plato himself thought that the moral effect of most kinds of poetry and music was bad.

their relations with one another, they achieve a harmony and a blending in the right proportions.[93] Then they bring abundance and well-being not only to humans but to all other animals and plant life, and do no harm. But whenever the other, violent sort of Love gains control of the seasons, he causes much destruction and harm. This is when plague and many other abnormal diseases tend to appear and afflict animals and plants. Frost, hail and blight arise from excess or disorder in the balance of such erotic influences. It is the knowledge of the relationship of these things to the movements of the heavenly bodies and the seasons of the year which we call astronomy.

188b

'Furthermore, all sacrifices and all matters that are the province of seers – that is to say, all the ways in which gods and men have dealings with one another – are entirely concerned with either the safeguarding or the cure of Love. For if, instead of gratifying and honouring the moderate Love and giving him pride of place in every enterprise, people honour the other Love, then every kind of impiety, towards parents living or dead as well as towards the gods, is likely to result. Indeed divination has been charged with the task of watching out for those who have this sort of love, and curing them. Divination is also the agent which brings about good relations between gods and humans because it knows what aspects of love in people's lives have an effect on correct religious behaviour.

188c

188d

'This is how great, how mighty, in short how complete the power of Love is in all his aspects. But it is the Love who is concerned with the good and finds fulfilment in it in company with temperance and justice, whether here on earth or among the gods, who has the greatest power and gives us all our happiness. It is he who enables us to associate and be friends with one another and with the gods, our masters.

188e

'Well now, I too may have passed over many things in my praise of Love, but if so it was not deliberate. If I have omitted anything it is up to you, Aristophanes, to fill the gap. However, if you have it in mind to praise the god in some other way, then proceed, and praise him, since you have got rid of your hiccups'.

Aristodemus said that Aristophanes duly took his turn. 'The hiccups have certainly stopped', he said, 'though not before I applied the sneezing cure. It surprises me that the good order[94] of one's body

189a

---

[93] 'in the right proportions' translates *sophron*; see *sophrosune*.
[94] A sly joke against Eryximachus' speech, hence the latter's sharp response.

desires the kind of ticklings and noises that make up a sneeze. When I resorted to sneezing the hiccups stopped immediately'.

'Watch what you are saying, my dear Aristophanes', said Eryximachus. 189b 'If you play the fool beforehand you force me to look out for more jokes during your speech as well, when you could speak without interruption'.

Aristophanes laughed and replied, 'Well said, Eryximachus, and please forget I spoke. There is no need for you to be on the look-out, because I am anxious enough on my own behalf about what I am going to say. My fear is not of being funny – that would be a bonus and very suitable for one of my profession – but of being ridiculous'.

'You think you'll get away with your barbed remarks, Aristophanes', Eryximachus said. 'But be careful and do not say what you cannot 189c justify later. Then perhaps I will decide to let you off'.

'In fact, Eryximachus', said Aristophanes. 'it is my intention to take a different line from you and Pausanias. It is my belief that people have entirely failed to understand the power of Love, for if they had understood they would have erected the greatest temples and altars to him and would offer up the largest sacrifices. As it is, nothing of the sort is done for him, though he deserves it more than anyone else. For he is 189d the most benevolent of gods to humankind, our helper and the healer of those ills whose cure would bring the greatest happiness to the human race. I am going to try to explain his power to you all, and then you in your turn can teach everyone else. In the first place you have to understand the nature of our human anatomy and what it has undergone. Once upon a time[95] our anatomy was quite different from what it is now. In the first place there were not merely two sexes as there are 189e now, male and female, but three, and the third was a combination of the other two. This sex itself has disappeared but its name, androgynous, survives. At that time the androgynous sex was distinct in form and name, having physical features from both the male and the female, but only the name now exists, and that as a term of insult.[96]

'Secondly, the form of every person was completely round, with back and sides making a circle, and with four arms, the same number of legs,

---

[95] Aristophanes' story, which resembles a folk-tale or a fable, is not known elsewhere.
[96] *androgunos.* For the Greeks generally it denoted not Aristophanes' creation but an effeminate or cowardly man.

and two faces exactly alike set on a round neck. There was one head for   190a
the two faces (which looked in opposite ways), four ears, two sets of
genitals and everything else as you might guess from these particulars.
They walked about upright, as we do today, backwards or forwards as
they pleased. Whenever they wanted to move fast they pushed off from
the ground and quickly wheeled over and over in a circle with their
eight limbs, like those acrobats who perform cartwheels by whirling
round with their legs straight out.

'The reason for the sexes being as they were and three in number is   190b
that originally the male was the offspring of the Sun, the female of the
Earth, and the androgynous of the Moon,[97] which shares the nature of
both Sun and Earth. Because they resembled their parents the offspring
themselves were round and their movement was circular also. They
were awesome in strength and might, and their ambition was great too.
They made an assault on the gods, and what Homer says about
Ephialtes and Otus[98] is said about these too, that they tried to make an
ascent to heaven in order to attack the gods.   190c

Zeus and the other gods deliberated about what they should do but
found no solution. They could hardly kill them and annihilate the
whole race with thunderbolts as they had the giants, for then they
would be putting an end also to the worship and sacrifices they received
from human beings, but neither could they put up with their insolence.
After much hard thought Zeus delivered his conclusion. 'I think I have
a plan', he said, 'that will allow humans to exist but at the same time put
an end to their outrageous behaviour by making them weaker. For the   190d
present I shall split each one of them in half, and that will make them
weaker, and at the same time they will be more useful to us by being
greater in number. They will walk upright on two legs, and if they
persist in their insolence and refuse to keep quiet I will split them in
half again, and they will have to hop about on one leg only'.

So saying he proceeded to cut everyone in two, just as people cut up
sorb-apples for preserving or slice eggs with a hair. As he divided them ·   190e
he told Apollo to take each separated half and turn round the face and
half neck to the cut side, so that each person by contemplating its own
cut surface might behave more moderately. He also told Apollo to heal

---

[97] See **Helios**, **Gaea** and **Selene** in Glossary of names.
[98] Mythical giants. See *Odyssey* 11, 305–20.

their wounds. So Apollo proceeded to turn the faces round and gathered the skin all together on the belly, as we now call it, like a purse with a drawstring, leaving one opening in the centre which he fastened with a knot, and which is now called the navel. He also smoothed out 191a most of the wrinkles and fashioned the chest, using a tool such as shoemakers use when they smooth out wrinkles in leather on the last. But he let a few wrinkles remain, around the belly and navel, to be a reminder of what happened ages ago.

'After the original nature of every human being had been severed in this way, the two parts longed for each other and tried to come together again. They threw their arms around one another in close embrace, 191b desiring to be reunited, and they began to die of hunger and general inactivity because they refused to do anything at all as separate beings. Whenever one of the two died and the other was left alone, the survivor would look for another mate to embrace, either the half of an original woman, as we now call it, or the half of a man. But in any case they were beginning to die out until Zeus took pity on them and thought up another plan: he moved their genital organs round to the front. Up until then they had their genitals on (what was originally) the outside of their 191c bodies, and conception and birth took place not in the body after physical union but, as with cicadas,[99] in the ground. By moving their genitals round to the front, Zeus now caused them to reproduce by intercourse with one another through these organs, the male penetrating the female. He did this in order that when couples encountered one another and embraced, if a man encountered a woman, he might impregnate her and the race might continue, and if a man encountered another man, at any rate they might achieve satisfaction from the union and after this 191d respite turn to their tasks and get on with the business of life.

'So it is that ever since that far-off time, love[100] of one person for another has been inborn in human beings, and its role is to restore us to our ancient state by trying to make unity out of duality and to heal our human condition. For each of us is a mere tally[101] of a person, one of two sides of a filleted fish, one half of an original whole. We are all continually searching for our other half. Those men who are sliced from originals

---

[99] It is not clear what Plato thought about the reproductive behaviour of cicadas.   [100] *eros.*
[101] A tally is one of two corresponding halves of a small object such as a coin or a dice (see 193a), one part being kept by each of two parties as proof of a transaction between them.

which comprised both sexes (formerly called androgynous) are lovers of women, and most adulterers originate from this sex, as do adulteresses and all women who are lovers of men. Women who are sliced from the wholly 191e female sex are not at all interested in men but are attracted towards other women, and female homosexuals come from this original sex. Men who are sliced from the wholly male original seek out males, and being slices of the male, while they are still boys they feel affection for[102] men and take pleasure in lying beside or entwined with them. In youth and young 192a manhood this sort of male is the best because he is by nature the most manly.[103] Some people say such males are without shame, but that is not true. They do what they do not out of shamelessness but out of confidence, courage and manliness, and they embrace that which is like themselves. And there is good evidence for this in the fact that only males of this type, when they are grown up, prove to be the real men in politics. Once they reach manhood, they become lovers of boys and are not natu- 192b rally inclined to marry or produce children, though they are compelled by convention. They are quite content to live out their lives with one another and not marry. In short, such a male is as a boy a lover of men, and as a man a lover of boys, always embracing his own kind.

'Now, whenever a lover of boys, or anyone else for that matter, meets his own actual other half, the pair are overcome to an extraordinary degree by sensations of affection,[104] intimacy[105] and love,[106] and they 192c virtually refuse to be parted from each other even for a short time. These are the couples who pass their whole lives together; yet they could not say what it is they want from one another. For no one would suppose it to be only the desire for love-making that causes the one to yearn for the other so intensely. It is clear that the soul of each wants something else which it cannot put into words but it feels instinctively 192d what it wants and expresses it in riddles. If the god Hephaestus, welding tools in hand, were to stand over them where they lie together, and ask, "What is it that you two want from each other?" they would be unable to answer. Suppose he were to ask them again, "Is this your desire,[107] to be always together, as close as possible, and never parted from each other day or night? If this is what you want, I am ready to join you together and fuse you until, instead of two, you become one. For your 192e

---

[102] *philein.* [103] or 'bravest'; see under *andreia.* [104] *philia*; see *philein.* [105] *oikeiotes.*
[106] *eros.* [107] *epithumein.*

whole lives long the two of you will live together as one, and when you
die you will die together and even in the Underworld you will be one
rather than two. Tell me if this is what you long for[108] and if it will
satisfy you to achieve this".

'We know that no one who heard these words would deny them or
would admit to wanting anything else. He would simply think that to
join with and melt into his beloved, so that instead of two they should
become one, was exactly what he had so long desired. The reason is that
our nature was originally like this and we were a whole, and the desire
193a and pursuit of the whole is called love. In the past, as I say, we were
one, but at the present time through our wrongdoing we have been
made by Zeus to live apart, as the Arcadians have been by the Spartans.[109] And if we are not well-behaved[110] towards the gods, the fear is
that we may be split up once more and go around looking like the
people you see in profile on monuments, sawn in half along the line of
the nose, or like the half-dice used as tallies.[111] For this reason we
should all promote reverence towards the gods in all things so as to
193b avoid the fate we do not want and obtain the one we do want, taking
Love as our guide and our leader. No one should oppose Love (and he
opposes him whoever is the enemy of the gods[112]). For if we become
friends and make our peace with the god then we shall find and join our
own particular beloved, which happens rarely at the present time.

'I hope Eryximachus won't treat my speech as comedy and take it
that I am alluding to Pausanias and Agathon. It may be that those two
193c really do belong to this category and are both wholly male in origin, but
I am actually talking about men and women everywhere when I say that
if we were to achieve that perfect love in which each of us meets his own
beloved and so returns to his original state, then the human race would
be happy. If this would be the best outcome of all, it follows that in the
present circumstances what comes nearest to this ideal is best; that is, to
find a beloved who is after one's own heart. If we are to praise the god

---

[108] *eran.*
[109] It is usually thought that this simile refers anachronistically to the dispersal by the Spartans of
the people of Mantinea in Arcadia to their original villages. Since the dispersal took place in
385 BC and is the latest datable event mentioned in the *Symposium*, it has been concluded by
most commentators that this is the earliest possible date for Plato's composition of the
dialogue. See Introduction footnote 3.
[110] *kosmioi*; see under *kosmos*.   [111] See footnote 101.
[112] The meaning of this obscure parenthesis is disputed.

who brings this about then it is Love that by rights we should praise. It 193d is Love who in the present confers on us the greatest benefit by leading us to that which is nearest to ourselves, and for the future gives us high hopes that if we show reverence to the gods, he will restore us to our original state, and heal us and make us blessed and happy.

'This is my speech about Love, Eryximachus', Aristophanes concluded, 'and very different from yours. As I asked you, please do not treat it as funny, but let us listen to what all the remaining speakers have to say, or rather, the other two: only Agathon and Socrates are left'.

'I shall heed what you say', said Eryximachus (according to 193e Aristodemus). 'In fact I found your speech most enjoyable. If I were not well aware that Socrates and Agathon are experts on the subject of love I should be very worried in case they would find nothing to say in view of the wide variety of things that have been said already. As it is, though, I am quite confident'.

'That is because you have already made your own successful con- 194a tribution, Eryximachus', said Socrates. 'If you were where I am now, or rather, where I shall be perhaps, when Agathon too has made a splendid speech, you would be very worried indeed and in the state of panic I am in now'.

'Your praise, Socrates, has a wicked purpose', said Agathon. 'You want to make me lose my head at the thought of the audience having high expectations of a great speech from me'.

'But I saw your assurance and confidence', Socrates replied, 'when 194b you went on to the platform with the actors and looked straight ahead at that huge audience without being in the least perturbed, and just before your own plays were to be performed too. I should have to be extremely forgetful to think you would lose your head now at the thought of a few people like us'.

'What do you mean, Socrates?' said Agathon. 'Surely you don't think me so obsessed by the theatre as not to realise that, to anyone with any sense, a small but thoughtful audience is far more terrifying than a large and thoughtless one?'

'Of course not, Agathon', he said. 'In your case I couldn't possibly 194c think anything so crass. I know very well that if you were faced with people you considered intelligent[113] you would take more notice of

---

[113] *sophos.*

them than of the general public. But after all, we too were there in the theatre and were part of the general public, so perhaps we are not these select few. However, if you did come across other people who were intelligent, you might well feel ashamed in front of them if you thought perhaps you were doing something wrong – what do you say?'

'You're right', he said.

'But in the case of the general public, you would not feel ashamed in front of *them* if you thought you were doing something wrong?'

194d   At this point, Aristodemus said, Phaedrus interrupted. 'My dear Agathon', he said, 'if you answer Socrates it won't matter to him any more if our arrangement comes to nothing so long as he has someone to talk to, especially someone good-looking. I enjoy hearing him talk myself but I also have to think about the encomium to Love and see that I get a speech from every one of you. So when the two of you have each rendered your due to the god, then you may have your discussion'.

194e   'Quite right, Phaedrus', said Agathon. 'There is nothing to prevent me making my speech, and there will be many future opportunities to talk to Socrates.

'I wish first to explain how my speech should proceed, and then to proceed with my speech.[114] All the earlier speakers seem to me not to have been eulogising the god but felicitating humans on the good things of which he is the source. But no one has described the nature of him

195a   who has bestowed these good things. Since the only proper way to make a eulogy of anyone is to describe first his nature and then the nature of the good things of which he is the source, so in the case of Love it is right for us to praise first his nature and then his gifts. Now, it is my contention that of those happy beings, the gods, the happiest of all – if they will allow me to say so without taking offence – is Love, because he is supreme in beauty and goodness.[115] He is the most beautiful in the

195b   following ways. First, Phaedrus, he is the youngest of the gods,[116] and he himself provides good evidence for what I say, for by his speed he outstrips old age, and everyone knows how fast old age advances; at any rate it comes upon us faster than it should. Love has a natural hatred of old age and never approaches anywhere near it. He always consorts with

---

[114] For the style see Gorgias in the Glossary of names.
[115] 'supreme in goodness' translates *aristos*; see *agathos*.
[116] Phaedrus had said he was the oldest, 178ab.

the young – "like goes with like", the old saying is right – so he is young himself. Therefore, much as I agree with Phaedrus in general, I cannot agree with him that Love is more ancient than those deities, Cronus and Iapetus. I say he is the youngest of the gods, and eternally young, and those bygone events among the gods which Hesiod and Parmenides relate, if they were telling the truth, happened through Necessity and not Love. For there would have been no castrations of gods or binding in chains or any other use of force if Love had already been among them. There would instead have been amity[117] and peace, as there is now, ever since Love has held sway over them.

'So, Love is young, and as well as being young he is tender. But he lacks a poet like Homer who can demonstrate his tenderness, as Homer does for Ate when he says that she is both a goddess[118] and tender – or her feet at least are tender:[119]

> "Tender are her feet, for not on the ground does she set them,
> But stepping on the heads of men she makes her way".

He seems to me to give clear evidence of her tenderness when he says that she does not walk on what is hard but only on what is soft, and we will use the same sort of evidence to show that Love too is tender. For Love does not walk on the ground, nor does he walk on the heads, for heads after all are not so very soft, but in the softest things there are he moves and lives, for he has set up his dwelling in the characters and souls of gods and humans. But not in every soul that presents itself, for whenever he encounters a soul with a hard and inflexible character he departs, but whenever he finds a soft character, there he lodges. Since he always fastens on to the softest of soft parts with his entire being, he must be very tender himself. So, then, he is very young and very tender, and he is supple in form as well. For if he were hard and inflexible he would not be able to enfold his object completely nor to pass unnoticed through the entire soul as he enters and leaves. Good evidence of his lithe and supple form is his gracefulness, which all agree Love possesses to an exceptional degree. For gracelessness and Love are always at war. Love spends his time among flowers: that is the reason

195c

195d

195e

196a

---

[117] *philia*; see *philein*.
[118] Ate means 'Infatuation', the divine personification of delusion. Sent by the gods as a punishment for a transgression, she entered into the minds of men so that they made disastrous decisions.
[119] *Iliad* 19. 92–3.

for the beauty of his complexion. But where there is no bloom of body
196b or soul or of anything else, or where the bloom has withered, there Love
does not alight; but where there is a place full of flowers and fragrance,
there he settles and remains.

'Concerning, then, the beauty of the god, though much remains unsaid,
that must suffice. It is concerning the virtue[120] of Love that I must now
speak. The most important thing is that Love does no injustice either to
god or man, and no injustice is done to him either by man or god. Anything
done to him is not done by force, and when he acts he does not act by force:
196c force and Love have nothing to do with each other. For everyone is in all
things the willing servant of Love, and whatever is agreed to by voluntary
consent, "the laws, the city's king"[121] declare to be just.

'In addition to justice, Love possesses self-control[122] in very large
measure. For all agree that self-control means overcoming pleasures
and desires, and also that no pleasure is stronger than Love. If, then,
pleasures are weaker, they will be overcome by Love, and Love will
overcome them, and if Love overcomes pleasures and desires, he must
be exceptionally self-controlled.

196d 'As for bravery, against Love "not even Ares can stand firm".[123] For
that god of war does not hold Love captive: Love has captured Ares –
love of Aphrodite that is to say – or so the story[124] goes. He who holds
captive is stronger than the one who is captured. And he who overcomes the bravest of all others must be himself the very bravest.

'Now, I have spoken about the justice and self-control and bravery of
the god; it remains for me to speak about his wisdom,[125] and I must try
as best I can not to fall short in my attempt. In the first place let me say
that the god is a skilful poet – in order that I too, like Eryximachus, may
196e pay honour to my craft[126] – and he is also able to make another person a
poet too. At any rate, at his touch every man becomes a poet "though
formerly unvisited by the Muse".[127] This we can properly take as
evidence that Love is a skilful creator in virtually every form of artistic
creation; for no one could give or teach another something which he

---

[120] *arete*; see footnote 72.
[121] A quotation from Alcidamas, a contemporary rhetorician.   [122] *sophrosune*.
[123] An altered line from the lost tragedy *Thyestes* by Sophocles. Agathon has substituted Love for
Necessity.
[124] The story is told by Homer in *Odyssey* 8. 266ff.
[125] *sophia*; in this context, poetic skill. See footnote 72.   [126] *techne*.
[127] A line from the lost tragedy *Stheneboea* by Euripides, meaning 'however unpoetical he was before'.

does not possess or know himself. And who will deny that it is by the   197a
wisdom of Love that all living things are begotten and born? Do we not
know that in the practice of a craft any man who has this god for
a teacher will turn out to be brilliant and famous, while the man
untouched by Love will remain obscure? Similarly it was under the
guidance of love and desire[128] that Apollo discovered archery and
medicine and divination, so that he too can be called a pupil of Love. So   197b
also the arts[129] of the Muses, the metal-work of Hephaestus, the
weaving of Athena and Zeus's governance of gods and men were all
learnt by those gods under the tutelage of Love. Thus the particular
interests of the gods were established only when Love had been born
among them, love of beauty obviously, since there is no love of ugliness.
Before that time, as I said at the start, many terrible deeds were done
among the gods, so the story goes, under the rule of Necessity. But ever
since this god was born, from the love of the beautiful every good thing
for gods and men has come into existence.

'So it is my belief, Phaedrus, that Love is not only supreme in beauty   197c
and goodness himself but is also the source of beauty and goodness in
all other things. Indeed, I feel I must speak about him in verse and say
that it is he who creates

> Peace among humankind, windless calm on the open sea,
> Rest for the winds and sleep in sorrow.

'It is Love who takes from us our sense of estrangement and fills us   197d
with a sense of kinship; who causes us to associate with one another as on
this occasion, and at festivals, dances and sacrifices is the guiding spirit.
He imparts gentleness, he banishes harshness; he is lavish with goodwill,
sparing of ill-will; he is gracious and kindly; viewed with admiration by
the wise and with wonder by the gods; coveted by those with no share of
him, precious to those whose share is large; the father of luxury, deli-
cacy, glamour, delight, desire and longing. He looks after good and cares
nothing for bad; in toil, in fear, in longing, in discourse, he is steersman,   197e
defender, comrade and saviour without compare, who confers order[130]
upon gods and humans alike, the finest and best guide, whom every man
should follow, singing beautiful hymns in his honour, taking part in the
song he sings to enchant the minds of all gods and humans alike.

---

[128] *epithumia.*   [129] *mousike.*   [130] *kosmos.*

'This, then, Phaedrus, is my speech, to be offered up to the god. I have made it playful in part but moderately serious too, to the best of my ability'.

198a   Aristodemus said that when Agathon finished speaking all the guests burst into applause, and everyone thought that the young man had spoken in a manner worthy of the god and of himself. Socrates turned to Eryximachus.

'Well, son of Acumenus, do you still think that my earlier fears were unfounded? Was I not a true prophet when I said just now that Agathon was going to deliver a brilliant speech and that I should be left with nothing to say?'[131]

'As far as Agathon's speech is concerned', replied Eryximachus, 'I accept that you spoke like a true prophet, but as for your having nothing to say, I think not'.

198b   'My dear man', exclaimed Socrates, 'how can I or anyone else not be left feeling that he has nothing to say, when he has to follow a discourse of such beauty and variety! The earlier parts were wonderful of course, but it was the final passage which must have stunned every listener with the beauty of its language. As I reflected that I would not be able to give a speech myself anywhere near as fine, I almost turned tail with shame – or would have done so if I could have escaped. The speech reminded

198c   me of Gorgias, so much so that I had the Gorgon experience as in Homer:[132] I was afraid Agathon would conclude his speech by challenging mine with the eloquence of Gorgias, that brilliant orator, and – like the Gorgon – would turn me into stone, unable to utter a word. It was then I realised what a fool I had been in agreeing with you to take

198d   my turn and deliver a eulogy of Love, and in saying I was an expert on the subject of love, despite, as it turned out, knowing nothing about how to compose a eulogy of anything. For in my naivety I thought I had only to speak the truth about the subject of the eulogy. This should be the foundation, I thought, and on the basis of the facts one selected the finest examples and arranged them to best effect. Assuming, then, that I knew the true way to eulogise, I even felt confident that I was going to

---

[131] See *aporein* in glossary.

[132] The reference is to *Odyssey* 11.634–5, where Odysseus retreats at the threat of the Gorgon's head. This is a punning joke based on the similarity of name between the mythological female monsters the Gorgons and the contemporary Sicilian Greek orator Gorgias, Agathon's stylistic exemplar. The head of the Gorgon Medusa turned to stone anyone who looked at it.

speak well. But actually, as it now appears, this is not the way to deliver a eulogy at all. Instead one should attribute to the subject the greatest and finest qualities possible whether they are truly there or not, and if what one says is not true, that doesn't matter. It now seems that the original proposal was not that each of us should really praise Love but that we should give the appearance[133] of doing so. This is the reason, I believe, that when you people attribute various qualities to Love, you go through all the stories that are told about him, and then declare that he is like this or like that and is the source of this good thing or that, in order to make him appear a paragon of beauty and goodness. This is obviously effective in the case of the ignorant, but surely not to those who know. And your praise certainly sounds fine and impressive. However, it seems I did not know how to make a eulogy, and it was in ignorance that I agreed to take my turn to eulogise. "My tongue it was that swore; my mind is not under oath".[134] Goodbye to my promise! I don't intend to eulogise in that way (for I could not do it); but if you like I am prepared to tell the truth about Love in my own fashion, though not in competition with your speeches; I do not want to be a laughing-stock. Phaedrus,[135] you might find out whether there is any call for a speech that entails listening to the truth about Love, spoken in whatever words and phrases happen to come into my head at the time'.

According to Aristodemus, Phaedrus and the others told Socrates to speak exactly as he thought he should.

'Then there is still one thing more, Phaedrus', said Socrates. 'Would you let me ask Agathon a few trivial questions, so that I can get his agreement on some points and then make my speech on that basis?'

'Of course', said Phaedrus. 'Ask away'. After that, according to Aristodemus, Socrates began at roughly the following point.

'I certainly thought you began your speech in the right way, my dear Agathon, when you said you had first to demonstrate what kind of being Love is, and then to proceed to his characteristic activity.[136] That is the sort of beginning I very much approve of. And since you have already

198e

199a

199b

199c

---

[133] See *doxa* in glossary.

[134] A notorious line (612) from the tragedy *Hippolytus* by Euripides, quoted here not altogether accurately.

[135] Phaedrus has taken on the role of master of ceremonies because the idea that Love should be eulogised originated with him. He had also prevented Socrates from questioning Agathon.

[136] 'characteristic activity' translates *erga* (plural of *ergon*; see glossary).

described in magnificent style what he is like, please tell me this further
199d thing: is Love such that he is love *of* something, or is he love *of* nothing?
(I don't mean "of" as in the question, "Is Love *the child of* some
particular mother or father?"[137] The question whether Love is love *of* a
mother or father in that sense would be ridiculous.) But suppose I asked
you about the essential meaning of the word "father", and whether
"father" was a father *of* something or not. To give the right answer you
would surely reply that "father" was a father *of* a son or *of* a daughter.
Isn't that so?'

'Of course', said Agathon.

'And you would say the same in the case of a mother?' Agathon
agreed.

199e 'Then perhaps you wouldn't object to answering a few more
questions', said Socrates, 'so that you will understand better what I
have in mind. If I were to ask you, "What about the essential meaning
of 'brother': is 'brother' a brother *of* something or is he not?" ' Agathon
said he was.

'Of a brother or a sister?'

'Yes'.

'Now', said Socrates. 'apply the same test to love. Is Love love *of*
something or is he love *of* nothing?'

'Certainly Love is love of something'.

200a 'Well then, keep this[138] in your mind, remembering what it is that
Love is love of', said Socrates, 'and for now tell me this: does Love
desire[139] that thing which he is love of, or not?'

'Certainly he desires it'.

'And does he desire and love it when he has in his possession that
thing which he desires and loves, or when he does not have it?'

'Probably when he does not have it', said Agathon.

---

[137] In Greek idiom, a statement in the form, 'Love is *of*' a person could mean that Love is '*the
child of*' that person. It seems that Socrates wants to make it clear that in his question he is not
interested in that use of 'of', but rather in the 'of' that introduces the object of love. Love
implies an object, just like other relationship words such as 'brother'. The Greek in the
manuscripts seems a little confused and may not be exactly what Plato originally wrote.

[138] Commentators are divided as to the meaning. The two possibilities are (1) that 'this' refers to
the conclusion just reached, and Agathon is then being asked in addition to remember that
earlier (at 197d) he had said that Love was love of beauty; and (2) that 'this' is an anticipatory
reference to the next clause and Agathon is being asked to keep in mind and remember only
what he has just agreed, namely that Love is love of something.

[139] *epithumein.*

34

'Now, instead of saying "probably"', said Socrates, 'consider whether it isn't *necessarily* true that that which desires, desires what it lacks, or, put another way, there is no desire if there is no lack. That seems to me, Agathon, an inescapable conclusion. What do you think?' 200b

'It seems so to me too'.

'Very good. So, would a man who was tall wish[140] to be tall, or a man who was strong wish to be strong?'

'From what has just been agreed that is impossible'.

'Exactly, because someone who has these attributes would not be lacking in them'.

'True'.

'But suppose', said Socrates, 'that a man who was already strong also wished to be strong, or a fast runner also wished to be fast, or a healthy man healthy: in these and all similar cases you might perhaps imagine that people who are like this and have these particular attributes also *desire* to have the attributes they have (and I am saying all this because I don't want us to get the wrong idea). If you think about it, Agathon, it must be the case that these people already possess their respective attributes whether they want to or not, and why would they also *desire* to have what they have? Therefore, when someone says, "I am healthy and I wish to be healthy", or "I am rich and I wish to be rich", or, "I desire exactly what I have", we will say to him, "My friend, you already possess wealth (or health or strength). What you really wish for is the continuing possession of these things in the future, for at the moment you have them whether you wish it or not". When you say, "I desire what I already have", consider whether you don't actually mean, "I wish I may continue to have in the future what I already have at present". Surely our friend would agree?' Aristodemus said that Agathon assented. 200c

200d

Socrates went on, 'So, then, he desires the possession and presence in the future of those things which he has at present. But isn't this equivalent to loving that thing which is not yet available to him and which he does not yet have? 200e

'Certainly it is'.

'Then this man and everyone who feels desire, desires what is not in his possession or presence, so that what he does not have, or what he is

---

[140] *boulesthai*.

35

not, or what he lacks, these are the sorts of things that are the objects of desire and love. Isn't this so?'

'Certainly'.

'Well now', said Socrates, 'let us sum up our conclusions so far. Isn't Love, first, *of* something, and, secondly, of something that he lacks?'

201a 'Yes'.

'On this basis, then, please recall what you said in your speech that Love was love of. I will remind you if you like. I think you said something like this, that the interests of the gods were established by reason of their love of beautiful things; for there is no love of ugly things, you said.[141] Didn't you say something like this?'

'Yes I did'.

'And reasonably enough, Agathon', said Socrates. 'And if this is the case, then surely Love is love of beauty and not of ugliness?'

Agathon agreed.

201b 'And we have already agreed that what he loves is what he lacks and does not possess?'

'Yes'.

'Then the conclusion is that what Love lacks and does not have is beauty'.

'That must be true'.

'And do you call a thing beautiful which lacks beauty and does not possess it in any respect?'

'Certainly not'.

'Then if this is so do you still say that Love is beautiful?'

To this Agathon replied, 'Socrates, it rather looks as though I understood nothing of what I was saying at the time'.

201c 'You spoke very well,[142] Agathon. Just one more small thing – doesn't what is good also seem to you beautiful?'

'Yes'.

'So if Love is lacking in what is beautiful, and what is good is beautiful, then he will also be lacking in what is good'.

'Socrates, I cannot argue against you, so let it be as you say'.

'There is no difficulty in arguing against Socrates, beloved Agathon; what you cannot argue against is the truth. But it is time I let you go.

---

[141] See 197b. [142] *kalos* (adverb); see glossary.

'Now I shall recount to you all a discourse about Love which I once 201d heard given by a woman from Mantinea, who was called Diotima.[143] She was an expert[144] on that subject and on many other subjects too. There was one occasion in particular, before the plague,[145] when she procured for the Athenians, after they had performed sacrifices, a ten-year postponement of that disease. She it was who taught me the whole subject of love, and it is the things she had to say about it that I shall try to recount to you, starting from the conclusions that Agathon and I reached together but speaking now on my own as best I can. As you demonstrated, Agathon, one should first define who Love is and what 201e he is like, before talking about his characteristic activity.

'I think it will be easiest to proceed as did my visitor from Mantinea with me on that occasion, by question and answer. I said much the same sort of things to her as Agathon said to me just now, that Love was a great god and that he was love of what is beautiful. She set about refuting[146] me with those arguments that I have just used against Agathon, demonstrating that according to my own account Love was neither beautiful nor good.

'And I protested. "What do you mean, Diotima? Are you actually saying Love is ugly and bad?"

"Watch what you say!" she exclaimed. "Do you really think that if something is not beautiful it has to be ugly?"

"I certainly do". 202a

"And something that is not wise is ignorant, I suppose? Have you not noticed that there is something in between wisdom[147] and ignorance?"

"And what is that?"

"Correct belief.[148] I am talking about having a correct belief without being able to give a reason for it. Don't you realise that this state cannot be called knowing – for how can it be knowledge[149] if it lacks reason? And it is not ignorance either – for how can it be ignorance if it has hit upon the truth? Correct belief clearly occupies just such a middle state, between wisdom[150] and ignorance".

---

[143] Probably a fictional character; see Glossary of names.   [144] *sophos.*
[145] Athens was struck by a devastating plague in 430 BC.   [146] See *elenchein.*   [147] *sophia.*
[148] *orthe doxa*; some translators and commentators translate as 'true belief' or 'right opinion'. All three translations mean the same thing.
[149] See under *epistasthai.*   [150] *phronesis.*

"That is true", I said.

202b   "Don't then insist that what is not beautiful has to be ugly, and what is not good has to be bad. Similarly with Love. When you yourself admit that Love is not good and not beautiful that is no reason for thinking he has to be ugly and bad. He is something between the two".

"At any rate surely everyone agrees that he is a great god".

"By 'everyone', she went on, "do you mean all who know, or do you include those who are ignorant?"

"I mean absolutely everyone".

'Then she laughed.

202c   "How could Love be acknowledged to be a great god by those who say he is not a god at all?"

"Who are they?" I asked.

"Why, you for one, and I for another".

"How can you say that?" I demanded.

"Easily", she replied. "Answer me this. Don't you say that all gods are happy and beautiful? Would you go so far as to say that any god was not?"

"No, by Zeus, I would not".

"And don't you mean by the happy those who are in possession of what is good and beautiful?"

"Certainly".

202d   "Yet in the case of Love you have agreed that it is through his lack of good and beautiful things that he desires those very things he lacks?"

"Yes, I have".

"So how could one be a god who has no portion of what is beautiful or good?"

"Not possibly, as it now appears".

"Do you see then", she said, "that you also do not believe that Love is a god?"

"In that case", I said, "what might Love be? Is he mortal?"

"No".

"What then?"

"As in the previous instances", she said, "something in between mortal and immortal".

"What is he then, Diotima?"

"He is a great spirit,[151] Socrates. All spirits are intermediate between 202e god and mortal".

"What is the function of a spirit?" I asked.

"Interpreting and conveying all that passes between gods and humans: from humans, petitions and sacrificial offerings, and from gods, instructions and the favours they return. Spirits, being intermediary, fill the space between the other two, so that all are bound together into one entity. It is by means of spirits that all divination can take place, the whole craft of seers and priests, with their sacrifices, rites 203a and spells, and all prophecy and magic. Deity and humanity are completely separate, but through the mediation of spirits all converse and communication from gods to humans, waking and sleeping, is made possible. The man who is wise in these matters is a man of the spirit,[152] whereas the man who is wise in a skill[153] or a manual craft,[154] which is a different sort of expertise, is materialistic.[155] These spirits are many and of many kinds, and one of them is Love".

"And who are his father and mother?" I asked.

"That is quite a long story", she said, "but I will tell you all the same. When Aphrodite was born,[156] all the gods held a feast. One of 203b those present was Poros[157] (Resource), whose mother was Metis[158] (Cleverness). When the feast was over, Penia (Poverty) came begging, as happens on these occasions, and she stood by the door. Poros got drunk on the nectar – in those days wine did not exist – and having wandered into the garden of Zeus was overcome with drink and went to sleep. Then Penia, because she herself had no resource, thought of a scheme to have a child by Poros, and accordingly she lay down beside him and became pregnant with a son, Love. Because Love was con- 203c ceived during Aphrodite's birthday feast and also because he is by his

---

[151] *daimon* (the source of English 'demon'), which can mean 'a god' but often denotes a lesser or local deity. Here Diotima characterises Love as a lesser deity, something between a god and a human. The Greeks of Plato's day would usually have thought of Love simply as a god, but not one of the most important, Olympian, deities. See Gods and Love in Glossary of names.

[152] *daimonios*, 'a man of the spirit', 'spiritual'; see footnote 151 above.

[153] *techne*. [154] *cheirourgia*. [155] *banausos* (English 'banausic').

[156] Diotima appears to follow the story that Aphrodite was the normally-born child of Zeus and Dione; see 180d and footnote 53. The rest of the narrative seems to be Plato's own invention.

[157] The Greeks commonly personified natural phenomena and in so doing made them into deities (often unimportant, as here). They sometimes explained them by constructing relationships between them, as is the case here with Poros and Penia.

[158] The first wife of Zeus and mother of Athena, the goddess of wisdom.

nature a lover of[159] the beautiful, and Aphrodite is beautiful, he has become her follower and attendant.

"However, since he is the son not only of Poros but also of Penia, he is in this position: he is always poor and, far from being the tender and beautiful creature that most people imagine, he is in fact hard and 203d rough, without shoes for his feet or a roof over his head. He is always sleeping on the bare ground without bedding, lying in the open in doorways and on the street, and because he is his mother's son, want is his constant companion. But on the other hand he also resembles his father, scheming to get what is beautiful and good, being bold and keen and ready for action, a cunning hunter, always contriving some trick or other, an eager searcher after knowledge,[160] resourceful, a lifelong lover 203e of wisdom,[161] clever with magic and potions, and a sophist.[162] His nature is neither that of an immortal nor that of a mortal, but in the course of a single day he will live and flourish for a while when he has the resources, then after a time he will start to fade away, only to come to life again through that part of his nature which he has inherited from his father. Yet his resources always slip through his fingers, so that although he is never destitute, neither is he rich. He is always midway between the two, just as he is between wisdom and ignorance.

204a   "The truth of the matter is this. No god pursues wisdom or desires to be wise because gods are wise already, and no one who is wise already pursues wisdom. But neither do ignorant people pursue wisdom or desire to be wise, for the problem of ignorance is this, that someone who is neither fine and good[163] nor wise[164] is still quite satisfied with himself. No one desires what he does not think he lacks".

"But who then are those who pursue wisdom, Diotima", I asked, "if they are neither the wise nor the ignorant?"

204b   "Even a child would know the answer to that by now", she replied. "It is those who are in between, and Love is one of them. For wisdom is

---

[159] Here and at 204b in the same phrase Diotima expresses 'love *of* beauty' by, unusually, the preposition *peri*, which more properly means 'love in the matter of the beautiful'. At 206e she is going to claim that Love is not simply 'of beauty' or 'of the beautiful' but 'of procreating and giving birth in the beautiful', thus refining what she had said at 203c and 204b. It would appear that in these two places Diotima uses *peri* rather than the simple 'of' so as not to commit herself.
[160] *phronesis.*   [161] 'Lover of wisdom' from *philosophein.*   [162] *sophistes.*   [163] *kalos kagathos.*
[164] *phronimos.*

a most beautiful thing, and Love is love of[165] the beautiful, so Love must be a philosopher,[166] and a philosopher is in a middle state between a wise man and an ignorant one. The reason for this too lies in his parentage: he has a father who is wise and resourceful, and a mother who is neither.

"This, then, is the nature of that particular spirit, my dear Socrates. But there was nothing surprising in the view you held yourself about the nature of Love. "Judging from what you say, I think you believed   204c that Love was that which is loved, not that which loves. This is the reason, I suppose, why Love appeared to you to be supremely beautiful. But in fact the one which is really beautiful and delicate, flawless and endowed with every blessing, is the beloved object, while the one which loves is by contrast of an entirely different character, such as I have just described".

"All right, Diotima", I replied. "You are very persuasive. If Love is as you say, what need does he supply in the lives of people?"

"That is the next thing I will try to teach you, Socrates", she said. "I   204d have just described Love's nature and parentage. Also, he is love of beautiful things, according to you. But what if someone asked us, 'What does it mean, Socrates and Diotima, to say that Love is love of beautiful things?' Or to put it more clearly: what does the lover[167] of beautiful things actually desire?[168]

"To possess them", I replied.

"But your answer raises yet another question: what will he gain by possessing beautiful things?"

'I said I certainly could not give a ready answer to that question.

"Well", she said, "suppose one changed the question and asked   204e about the good instead of the beautiful: 'Come now, Socrates, what does the lover of good things actually desire?'"

"To possess the good things", I replied.

"And what will he gain if he possesses them?"

"Ah, that is an easier question to answer: he will be happy".

"Yes", she replied. "The happy are happy through the possession   205a of good things, and there is no need to ask further why anyone wishes

---

[165] *peri*; see footnote 159.   [166] *philosophos*; see *philosophein*.

[167] *ho eron*, 'the one who loves'; see *eran*.

[168] 'desire', from *eran*, which means both 'to love' and, as here, 'to feel desire for'. Similarly in the case of the noun, 'love of' can mean 'desire for'.

to be happy. That answer seems to have brought the matter to a conclusion".[169]

"True", I said.

"About this wish, this desire – do you think it is common to all? Do all humans wish always[170] to possess good things, or what?"

"Yes", I replied, "it is as you say a wish common to all".

"Why is it, then, Socrates, that if in fact all people always love the same things we do not describe all people as being in love, instead of saying that some are and that others are not?"

205b

"I wonder about that myself", I replied.

"There is no need to wonder", she said. "The reason is that we are picking out one particular kind of love and giving it the name which applies to all, but for the other kinds of love we use different names".

"Can you give me another example?" I asked.

"Yes, there is this one. You realise that the word 'poetry' [originally meant 'creation' and that 'creation'][171] is a term of wide application. When something comes into existence which has not existed before, the whole cause of this is 'creation'. The products of every craft are creations and the craftsmen who make them are all creators".[172]

205c

"That is so".

"But you also know", she went on, "that they are not all called creators. They have other names, and only that one part of creation which is separated off from the rest and is the part that is concerned with song and verse is called by the original name of the whole class, which is poetry, and only those to whom this part of creation belongs are called poets".

"That is so".

205d "Well, the same is true of love. In general the truth is that for everyone, all desire for good things and for being happy[173] is 'guileful and most mighty love'.[174] People who turn to love in one of its many other forms – money-making or athletics or philosophy – are not then

---

[169] *telos.* See glossary.

[170] Greek word order, sometimes ambiguous, suggests here that 'always' goes with 'wishes' rather than 'possess', but the proximity of 'always' and 'possess' prepares the reader for Diotima saying at the end of 206a that love is the desire to possess the good always.

[171] The words in brackets are not in the Greek but are needed in the translation because modern English has no word equivalent to Greek *poiesis*, which means both 'poetry' and 'creation'.

[172] *poietai*; see *poiesis*.   [173] *eudaimonein.*

[174] Apparently a poetic quotation, from a source unknown to us.

called 'lovers' or said to be 'in love'. It is only those who ardently pursue one particular form who attract those terms which should belong to the whole class: they alone feel 'love', or are 'in love', or are 'lovers'.

"You are very probably right", I said.

"Yes, and you will hear it said that lovers are people who are looking   205e
for their own other half. But what I say, my friend, is that love is not directed towards a half, or a whole either, unless that half or whole is actually something good, since people are quite prepared to have their own hands or feet amputated if they believe that these parts of themselves are diseased. So it is not, I think, part of themselves that people cling to, unless there is someone who calls what belongs to him and is his own the good and what does not belong to him the bad. The fact is that the only   206a
thing people love is the good. Do you think there is anything else?"

"By Zeus, there is nothing else", I said.

"Well then", she went on, "can we say without qualification that people love the good?"

"Yes", I replied.

"But shouldn't we add that what they love is that the good should be theirs?"

"We should".

"And not only that", she said, "but that the good should always be theirs?"

"Yes, we must add that too".

"Then we can sum up", she said. "Love is the desire to possess the good always".

"That is very true".

"Then since this is always what love is", she said, "can you tell me   206b
how those who pursue it go about it? What are they doing that the zeal and drive they show can be called love? What does this activity[175] really consist of? Can you say?"

"If I knew the answer, Diotima", I replied, "I wouldn't be so admiring of you for your wisdom, or coming to you to learn these very things".

"Then I shall tell you", she said. "It is giving birth in the beautiful, in respect of body and of soul".

"I need an interpreter to tell me what you mean", I said. "I don't understand".

[175] *ergon.*

43

206c   "Then I shall speak more clearly", she replied. "All human beings are pregnant,[176] Socrates, in body and in soul, and when we reach maturity it is natural that we desire to give birth. It is not possible to give birth in what is ugly,[177] only in the beautiful. I say that because the intercourse of a man and a woman[178] is a kind of giving birth. It is something divine, this process of pregnancy and procreation. It is an aspect of immortality in the otherwise mortal creature, and it cannot

206d take place in what is discordant. Now, the ugly is not in accord with anything divine, whereas the beautiful accords well. So at this birth Beauty takes on the roles of Fate and Eileithyia.[179] For this reason, whenever the pregnant being approaches the beautiful, it is in favourable mood. It melts with joy, gives birth and procreates. In the face of ugliness, however, it frowns and contracts with pain, and shrivelling up it fails to procreate, and it holds back its offspring in great suffering. This is the reason why, for a pregnant being now ready to give birth,

206e there is much excitement at the presence of the beautiful because its possessor will deliver the pregnant one from great pain. For the object of love, Socrates", she said, "is not, as you think, simply the beautiful".

"What, then?"

"It is procreating and giving birth in the beautiful".

"All right", I said.

"It certainly is", she replied. "But why is the object of love procreation? Because procreation is a kind of everlastingness and

207a immortality for the mortal creature, as far as anything can be. If the object of love is indeed everlasting possession of the good, as we have already agreed, it is immortality together with the good that must necessarily be desired. Hence it must follow that the object of love is also immortality".

'All these things Diotima taught me on the occasions when she spoke about love. On one occasion she asked me, "What do you think, Socrates, is the cause of this love and desire? Do you not notice what a

---

[176] Diotima uses the language of sexual intercourse and birth to describe the feelings and sexual activity mainly of the male. On the images of pregnancy and procreation see F. Sheffield, 'Psychic Pregnancy and Platonic Epistemology', *Oxford Studies in Ancient Philosophy* XX (summer 2001), 1–35.

[177] *aischros.*

[178] Some Greeks believed that women too emitted a kind of seminal fluid at the moment of conception.

[179] The goddess of childbirth.

state all beasts are in, birds as well as four-footed animals, when they feel the desire to procreate? All sick and in the grip of love, they are 207b concerned first for copulation and then for rearing the offspring, and they are ready to fight it out on their behalf, the weakest against the strongest, even to the death, worn out themselves by hunger in the attempt to feed them, yet ready to do whatever else is necessary. One might suppose that humans do these things because they reason about it. But animals – what cause is there for them to be so affected by love? Can you tell me why?" 207c

'Again I replied that I did not know. She retorted, "And do you suppose you will ever become expert on the subject of love if you are not going to think about this matter?"

"But Diotima, as I said just now, it is precisely because I recognise that I need teachers that I have come to you. Just tell me the reason for this and for everything else to do with love".

"Well then", she said, "if you believe that love is by its nature directed towards that thing which we have agreed upon many times, you should not be surprised. For in the animal world and among humans the same explanation applies, that mortal nature seeks as far as 207d it can to exist for ever and to be immortal. But the only way it can achieve this is by continual generation,[180] the process by which it always leaves behind another new thing to replace the old. Consider the time when any living thing is described as being alive and being the same individual – as a man, for example, is said to be the same person from childhood until old age. Although he is referred to as the same person, he never keeps the same constituents; he is always being renewed, while things like hair, flesh, bones, blood – in fact the entire body – are constantly passing away. This happens not only in the body but also in 207e the soul. A soul's habits, characteristics, beliefs, desires, pleasures, pains, fears, none of these things ever remain constant in an individual, but some are always coming into being while others pass away. Stranger still is the situation with the various branches of our knowledge.[181] Not 208a only do they too come and go, so that we do not remain the same in the case of them either, but it is also true of each single thing we know. Consider what we call revising or practising.[182] We do this because knowledge leaves us. Forgetting is the loss of knowledge, and revising,

[180] *genesis.*   [181] see under *epistasthai.*   [182] 'revising or practising' translates *melete*; see glossary.

45

by implanting a fresh memory in place of the one that is departing, preserves our knowledge so that it seems to be the same. In this way everything mortal is preserved, not by remaining entirely the same for

208b   ever, which is the mark of the divine, but by leaving behind another new thing of the same kind in the place of what is growing old and passing away. By this means, Socrates", she said, "what is mortal-body and every creature else-partakes of immortality; but what is immortal does so differently. So do not be surprised that everything naturally values its own offspring. This universal zeal and love is for the sake of immortality".

I was surprised to hear this speech. "Well now, Diotima", I said. "I

208c   know you are very wise, but is this really how things are?" Like the perfect sophist[183] she replied: "Believe me, Socrates. You have only to look at humankind's love of honour and you will be surprised at your absurdity regarding the matters I have just mentioned, unless you think about it and reflect how strongly people are affected by the desire to become famous and 'to lay up immortal glory for all time'.[184] For the sake of this they are prepared to run risks even more than for their children – spend their money, endure any kind of suffering, even die in

208d   the cause. Do you suppose", she went on, "that Alcestis would have died to save Admetus, or Achilles would have sacrificed his life to avenge Patroclus, or your Athenian king Codrus would have perished before his time for the sake of his sons' succession, if they had not thought that the memory of their virtue,[185] which indeed we still have of them, would be immortal? Far from it", she said. "I think that it is for the sake of immortal fame[186] and this kind of glorious reputation[187] that everyone strives to the utmost, and the better they are the more

208e   they strive: for they desire what is immortal.

"Those whose pregnancy is of the body", she went on, "are drawn more towards women, and they express their love through the pro-creation of children, ensuring for themselves, they think, for all time to come, immortality and remembrance and happiness in this way. But [there are][188] those whose pregnancy is of the soul – those who are

209a   pregnant in their souls even more than in their bodies, with the kind of

---

[183] Perhaps the confidence of her answer was thought characteristic of sophists (see *sophistes*).
[184] A line of poetry from an unknown source.   [185] Or 'courage'; see *arete*.
[186] *arete*.   [187] *doxa*.   [188] The verb supplied is missing in the Greek.

offspring which it is fitting for the soul to conceive and bear. What offspring are these? Wisdom[189] and the rest of virtue,[190] of which the poets are all procreators, as well as those craftsmen who are regarded as innovators. But by far the most important and beautiful expression of this wisdom is the good ordering[191] of cities and households; and the names for this kind of wisdom are moderation and justice.

"When someone has been pregnant in soul with these things from youth and is of the right age but unmarried,[192] he now feels the desire to give birth and procreate. He too, I think, goes about looking for the beautiful in which to procreate; for he will never procreate in the ugly. In his pregnant state he welcomes bodies that are beautiful rather than ugly, and if he comes across one who has a beautiful, noble and gifted soul as well, then he particularly welcomes the combination. In the presence of this person his words immediately flow in abundance about virtue and about the qualities and practices that make for a good man, and he embarks on his education. For I think that by attaching himself to the beautiful and associating with it, which he will be keeping in mind even when absent, he gives birth to and procreates the offspring with which he has long been pregnant, and in company with that other share in nurturing what they have created together. The result is that such a couple have a much closer partnership with each other and a stronger tie of affection than is the case with the parents of mortal children, since the offspring they share in have more beauty and immortality. For anyone who looked at Homer and Hesiod and all the other great poets would envy them because of the kind of offspring they have left behind them, and would rather be the parent of children like these, who have conferred on their progenitors immortal glory and fame, than of ordinary human children.

"For another example", she said, "look at the sort of children Lycurgus[193] left behind in Sparta to be the salvation of Sparta and, one might say, of Greece itself. And Solon[194] too is honoured by you

---

[189] *phronesis.*   [190] See footnote 72.   [191] *diakosmesis*; see under *kosmos.*

[192] This word in Greek, *ëitheos*, is an editor's emendation of the manuscripts' *theos*, 'divinely inspired'; in the view of other editors the reading 'divinely inspired' makes better sense.

[193] Lycurgus was the legendary founder of the Spartan legal and military systems. The defeat of the invading Persians by the Spartan army in the Persian Wars could be said to have saved Greece from conquest in the early fifth century BC. For **Lycurgus** see Glossary of names.

[194] Solon's constitutional reforms at Athens in the early sixth century BC paved the way for the development of democracy in that city state. See Glossary of names.

209e Athenians as the procreator of your laws, and other men are similarly honoured in many other places in Greece and beyond, who by their many fine achievements have procreated virtue of every kind. Many sacred cults have been set up in their honour because of the nature of those children, but none has ever yet been set up because of mortal children.

"These are aspects of the mystery of love[195] that perhaps you too, 210a Socrates, might be initiated into. But for the final initiation and revelation, to which all this has been merely preliminary for someone on the right track, I am not sure if you have the capability. However I will do my utmost to explain to you, and you must try to follow if you can.

"A person who would set out on this path in the right way must begin in youth by directing his attention to beautiful bodies, and first of all, if his guide is leading him aright, he should fall in love with the body of one individual only, and there procreate beautiful discourse. Then he will realise for himself that the beauty of any one body is 210b closely akin to that of any other body, and that if what is beautiful in form[196] is to be pursued it is folly not to regard the beauty in all bodies as one and the same. When he has understood this he should slacken his intense passion for one body, despising it and considering it a small thing, and become a lover of all beautiful bodies.

"After this he will realise that the beauty in souls[197] is more to be prized than that in the body. If therefore someone's soul is good even if his physical attraction is slight, that will be enough for him, and he will love and care for that person, and seek out and give birth to the kind of 210c discourse that will make young men better people. As a consequence he will be compelled to contemplate the beautiful as it exists in human practices and laws, to see that the beauty of it all is of one kind, and to realise that what is beautiful in a body is trivial by comparison.

"After this his guide must lead him to contemplate knowledge in its various branches, so that he can see beauty there too, and looking at 210d what is now a wide range of beauty he is no longer slavishly content with the beauty of any one particular thing, such as the beauty of a young boy or some other person, or of one particular practice, and will

---

[195] *erotica*. Diotima is speaking as if Socrates was now reaching the final stages of initiation into a religious mystery-cult. See **Mysteries** in Glossary of names.
[196] *eidos*. See glossary. [197] *psuche*.

not become petty and small-minded through this kind of servitude. Instead he will turn towards the vast sea of the beautiful and while contemplating it he will give birth to many beautiful, indeed magnificent, discourses and thoughts in a boundless love of wisdom until there, strengthened and invigorated, he discerns a unique kind of knowledge, which is knowledge of a beauty whose nature I will now describe. And please try to pay attention as closely as you can", she went on. 210e

"Anyone who has been guided to this point in the study of love and has been contemplating beautiful things in the correct way and in the right sequence, will suddenly perceive, as he now approaches the end of his study, a beauty that is marvellous in its nature – the very thing, Socrates, for the sake of which all the earlier labours were undertaken. What he sees is, in the first place, eternal; it does not come into being or 211a perish, nor does it grow or waste away. Secondly, it is not beautiful in one respect and ugly in another, or beautiful at one time and not at another, or beautiful by one standard and ugly by another, or beautiful in one place and ugly in another because it is beautiful to some people but ugly to others. Nor, again, will the beautiful appear to him as a face is beautiful or hands or any other part of the body, nor like a discourse or a branch of knowledge or anything that exists in some other thing, whether in a living creature or in the earth or the sky or anything else. It 211b exists on its own, single in substance[198] and everlasting. All other beautiful things partake of it, but in such a way that when they come into being or die the beautiful itself does not become greater or less in any respect, or undergo any change.

"Now, whenever someone starts to ascend from the things of this world through loving boys in the right way, and begins to discern that beauty, he is almost in reach of the goal. And the correct way for him to go, or be led by another, to the things of love,[199] is to begin from the 211c beautiful things in this world, and using these as steps, to climb ever upwards for the sake of that other beauty, going from one to two and from two to all beautiful bodies, and from beautiful bodies to beautiful practices, and from beautiful practices to beautiful kinds of knowledge,[200] and from beautiful kinds of knowledge finally to that particular

---

[198] *monoeides*; literally, 'in single form'.
[199] *erotica*. See glossary.
[200] *mathemata* (plural) is used here rather than *episteme*. See glossary.

knowledge which is knowledge solely of the beautiful itself, so that at
211d last he may know what the beautiful itself really is. That is the life, my
dear Socrates", said the visitor from Mantinea, "which most of all a
human being should live, in the contemplation of beauty itself".

"If ever you see that beauty, it will not seem to you to be comparable
with gold or dress or those beautiful boys and young men who now
drive you and many others to distraction when you see them. If only
you could see your beloveds and be with them all the time you would be
prepared – if only it were possible – to go without food and drink, and
do nothing but gaze at them and be with them. What, then, do we
211e suppose it would be like", she said, "for someone actually to see the
beautiful itself, separate, clear and pure, unsullied by the flesh or by
colour or by the rest of our mortal dross, but to perceive the beautiful
itself, single in substance and divine? Do you think", she continued,
212a "that a person who directs his gaze to that object and contemplates it
with that faculty by which it has to be viewed,[201] and stays close to it,
has a poor life? Do you not reflect", she went on, "that it is there alone,
when he sees the beautiful with that by which it has to be viewed, that
he will give birth to true virtue? He will give birth not to mere images of
virtue but to true virtue, because it is not an image that he is grasping
but the truth. When he has given birth to and nurtured true virtue it is
possible for him to be loved by the gods and to become, if any human
can, immortal himself".

212b   'Well, Phaedrus and all of you, these are the things that Diotima said
to me, and I believe her. And since I believe, I am trying to persuade
everyone else that in the attainment of this goal human nature could not
easily find a better helper than Love. For this reason I declare for my
part that every man should honour Love, and I myself honour the study
of love and practise it to an exceptional degree. I urge everyone else
to do likewise, and now and ever I praise the power and bravery of
212c Love as best I can. So, Phaedrus, consider this speech, if you will, as my
encomium to Love, or, if you prefer, call it whatever you please'.

With these words Socrates concluded his speech. Aristodemus said
that everyone was praising it, and Aristophanes was trying to say something about the reference Socrates had made to his own speech, when

---

[201] Plato in *Republic* 533d calls this faculty 'the eye of the soul' (*psuche*); it is elsewhere associated
with *nous*, mind or intellect.

suddenly there was a loud banging on the outside door. It sounded like a party of revellers, and they could hear a girl playing the *aulos*. 'Go and see who it is', said Agathon to the servants, 'and if it is one of my friends, ask him in, but if not say that the drinking is over and we are calling a halt'. 212d

Not long after, the voice of Alcibiades was heard in the courtyard; he was very drunk and shouting loudly, asking where Agathon was and demanding to be taken to Agathon. So Alcibiades was ushered in, supported by some of his attendants and the girl who played the *aulos*. 212e He stood by the door, crowned with a bushy garland of ivy and violets and with an abundance of ribbons tied round his head. 'Good evening, gentlemen', he said. 'Will you welcome as a fellow drinker a man already very drunk, or must I merely crown Agathon, which is what I came for, and then go away again? For I have to tell you', he said, 'I couldn't come yesterday, but here I am now with ribbons on my head, to put this crown from my own head on to the head of the wisest and handsomest man, and proclaim him to be so. Will you laugh at me 213a because I am drunk? You may laugh, but all the same I know my proclamation is true. But tell me straight away: do you agree to my terms? May I come in or not? Will you drink with me or not?'

Everyone shouted assent, telling him to come in and take a place, and Agathon invited him to join them. So in he came, escorted by his companions. Because he was simultaneously untying the ribbons in order to crown Agathon with them and had them in front of his eyes, he did not notice Socrates, who, catching sight of him, had moved over. Alcibiades sat down beside Agathon, between him and Socrates, and as 213b he did so he embraced Agathon and crowned him.

'Take off Alcibiades' shoes', said Agathon to the servants, 'so that he can have the third place on the couch'.

'Thank you', said Alcibiades, 'but who is this on my other side?' As he spoke, he turned round and saw Socrates. At once he leaped up. 'Heracles!' he exclaimed, 'What is this! *You*, Socrates? You were lying there to ambush me again, just as you used to do, making a sudden 213c appearance in a place where I least expected you. Now what are you up to? And another thing, why are you on this particular couch? I notice you are not beside someone like Aristophanes who enjoys mockery too. No, you have schemed to take a place beside the best-looking man in the room'.

'Agathon, keep him off, please', cried Socrates. 'I must say my passion for him has become quite a burden. From the moment I fell in
213d love with him I have not been allowed to look at or talk to a single good-looking man, or if I do so this man here gets jealous and resentful and his behaviour is quite extraordinary – he hurls insults at me and all but hits me. Take care he doesn't do something like this now. Do keep the peace between us, or if he tries to use force, protect me, because I am completely terrified by his mad obsession with being loved'.

'No peace is possible', said Alcibiades, 'between the two of us, and I will take my revenge for these allegations later on. But as for now,
213e Agathon, please give me back some of the ribbons to crown this man's head too, this wonderful head of his, so that he cannot blame me for crowning you and not him. When it is a contest of words he beats every one else, not just once, like you the day before yesterday, but every time'. So saying he took some of the ribbons and crowned Socrates, and then took his place on the couch.

When he had settled himself he spoke again. 'Well now, gentlemen, you seem to me to be quite sober. This must not be allowed; you have to drink. We have made an agreement. So for our master of ceremonies, until you have all drunk adequately, I elect – myself. Agathon, get someone to bring a really big cup, if you have one. No, there is no need.
214a Boy, bring me that wine-cooler there', he ordered, seeing that it held more than eight cotylae.[202] Having had this filled Alcibiades first drained it himself, then told them to fill it again for Socrates, saying as they did so, 'In the case of Socrates, gentlemen, my trick is useless. However much you provide, he will drink it all and never be drunk'.

So the servant filled the wine-cooler again and Socrates was drinking from it when Eryximachus spoke. 'How are we arranging things, then, Alcibiades?' he asked. 'Are we not going to have conversation or singing
214b as the wine goes round? Are we simply going to drink like thirsty men?'

'O Eryximachus', said Alcibiades, 'best son of the best and most sober[203] father, my greetings to you'.

'And the same to you. But what should we do?'

'Whatever you say, and we must obey you. For "one learned leech is worth an army of laymen".[204] Therefore prescribe as you please'.

---

[202] A cotylē measures nearly half a pint (or quarter of a litre).   [203] *sophron*.
[204] Homer, *Iliad* 11. 514; the translation is adapted from that of R.G. Bury.

'All right, then', said Eryximachus. 'Listen and I will tell you. Before you arrived we had decided that each of us should make as fine a speech as possible in praise of Love, going from left to right in turn. Since all 214c the rest of us have spoken while you, on the other hand, have drunk all your wine but not yet spoken, you are entitled to speak, and afterwards you can give Socrates any instruction you like. He can do the same to the man on his right, and so on'.

'That is all very well, Eryximachus', said Alcibiades, 'but for a drunken man to be in competition with the speeches of the sober is scarcely fair. And another thing, my dear friend: do you really believe 214d what Socrates said just now? Do you realise that the truth is entirely the opposite of what he was saying? *He* is the one who starts hitting *me* if I try to praise anyone else, god or man, in his presence'.

'Watch what you say!' said Socrates.

'By Poseidon!' exclaimed Alcibiades, 'You cannot deny that! I would never praise anyone else in your presence'.

'In that case', said Eryximachus, 'go ahead if you want to, and praise Socrates'.

'What's that?' said Alcibiades. 'Do you think I should, Eryximachus? 214e Can I really take on this man and get my revenge in front of you all?'

'Here, you, wait a bit!' cried Socrates. 'What do you have in mind? Will you praise me just for everyone's amusement, or what?'

'I shall speak the truth. Are you going to let me?'

'If it is the truth I will certainly let you. In fact I insist on it'.

'I will start at once', said Alcibiades. 'However, you must do this for me. If I say anything that is not true, please interrupt and tell me that I am mistaken, because I certainly do not intend to say what is untrue. On 215a the other hand don't be surprised if I get events mixed up when I try to remember them. It's not all that easy for someone in my condition to list the particulars of your unusual nature fluently and in the right order.

'The method of praising Socrates that I shall adopt, gentlemen, is to make comparisons. My subject here will perhaps think I am doing this for amusement but my comparisons will be for the sake of truth, not just to amuse. It is my contention that he is very like those sileni[205] that

---

[205] Sileni were minor nature deities, like satyrs, portrayed in Greek art with snub noses and bulging eyes, and so looking like Socrates, it was commonly said. See **Satyrs** in Glossary of names.

215b you find in statuaries' workshops which the craftsmen make holding
      pipes or *auloi*, and when you open them up you see that they contain
      small statues of the gods inside. I say also that he is like the satyr
      Marsyas in particular. Not even you, Socrates, could dispute the fact
      that you are like these creatures in appearance, and now you are going
      to hear how you are like them in other ways too. You treat people
      insolently.[206] Isn't that true? If you don't admit it I will produce wit-
      nesses. But you are not an *aulos*-player, you say? Yes you are, and a
215c much more amazing player than Marsyas. Marsyas used to charm
      everyone with his pipes through the power that came from his mouth,
      and we are still charmed today whenever we hear his music played. I say
      "his" because I ascribe to Marsyas the melodies that Olympus used to
      play, because it was Marsyas who taught Olympus. In the case of
      Olympus's music, whether it is played by a great performer or by an
      ordinary *aulos*-girl, it takes hold of men in a unique way and, because of
      its divine origin, it reveals those who are in need of the gods and of
      initiation rites.[207] Now you, Socrates, differ from Marsyas only in this:
      you achieve the same effect with simple prose rather than with pipes.
215d For instance, when we hear someone holding forth on some topic or
      other, even if he is a very good speaker, he has virtually no effect on us.
      But whenever we hear you speaking or hear your words repeated by
      someone else, however mediocre the speaker may be, still we are all –
      woman, man or child alike – spellbound and entranced. In my own case,
      for example, were it not for the risk of sounding the worse for drink, I
      would have told you gentlemen on oath how I have been affected by this
215e man's words, and how I am still affected even now. Whenever I listen
      to him I am more upset than those driven to frenzy by the Cory-
      bantes.[208] My heart pounds and tears flow, merely because of this man's
      words, and I notice that very many others too are affected in the same
      way. When I used to listen to Pericles and other great orators I naturally
      thought they spoke well, but I was never affected to anything like the

---

[206] See glossary under *hubrizein*. The insolence of satyrs took the form of drunken violence and
      sexual assault, whereas that of Socrates was perceived by his victims (usually his interlocutors)
      to be his sarcastic or ironic attitude towards them, which made them feel that, rather like the
      victims of unprovoked assault, they were being treated with contempt.

[207] Initiation into a mystery religion; Olympus's music had a diagnostic effect, we are being told,
      on those whose minds were disturbed.

[208] Votaries of a mystery religion. They were noted for their wild dances and music which had a
      cathartic and so curative effect on the mentally disturbed.

same extent. My soul wasn't in turmoil, and I wasn't disturbed by the thought that I was a slave to my way of living. But after listening to this Marsyas here I was very often reduced to thinking that being as I was, 216a my kind of life was not worth living. And this, Socrates, you will not deny.

'I am still very well aware that if I allowed myself to listen to him I would not be able to hold out and I would be affected in exactly the same way. For he compels me to admit that even with all my deficiencies I nevertheless take no care for myself, but instead I involve myself in the concerns of the Athenians. So I stop my ears to his Siren song and force myself to run away so as not to spend the rest of my life sitting here at his side. What I have felt in the presence of this one man is what no one 216b would think I had it in me to feel in front of anyone, and that is shame. And it is only in front of him that I feel it, because I am well aware that I cannot argue against him or deny that I ought to do as he says. Yet when I leave him I am equally aware that I am giving in to my desire for honour from the public. So I skulk out of his sight like a runaway slave, and whenever I do see him I am ashamed of the admissions I have made to him. There have been many occasions when I would have been glad to 216c see him disappear from the land of the living; but if that were to happen I know that I would be far more grieved than glad. The consequence is that I have no idea how to deal with this person.

'That, then, is the effect that the music of this particular satyr has had on me and on many others as well. Now I am going to tell you the other ways in which he resembles those I have been comparing him with, and about the astonishing power that he has. Bear in mind that none of you really knows this man; but now that I have started, I will reveal him to you. What you see is a Socrates who is liable to fall in love 216d with beautiful young men, is always in their company and is greatly taken by them. And then again he is also completely ignorant and knows nothing – so far as outward appearance goes. Is this not silenus-like? Of course it is. On the surface you see the moulded form of the silenus. But on the inside, once he has been opened up, you can't imagine, my fellow-drinkers, how much self-control is to be found within. Believe me, he is not a bit interested in whether someone is good-looking, and in fact he despises good looks more than you would ever imagine. The 216e same is true of wealth and every other mark of distinction that most people regard as a matter for congratulation. He considers that all these attributes are worthless and that we ourselves – I mean it – are of no account. He spends his whole life pretending ignorance[209] and teasing people. But when he is in a serious mood and opened up I don't know if anyone else has seen the statues he has inside, but I saw them once, and they seemed to me so divine and golden, so utterly beautiful and wonderful, that in brief I felt I had to do whatever Socrates told me to do.

217a

'So, when I thought he had become seriously interested in my youthful good looks, I considered this a godsend and a piece of amazing good fortune for me because it gave me the opportunity, in gratifying him, to hear from him everything he knew. For I was incredibly vain about my looks. Hitherto it had not been my practice to be with him alone and unaccompanied, but when I had formed my plan I started dismissing my attendant and I would be there in Socrates' company by myself (I have to tell you the whole truth, so please pay attention and, Socrates, if I say anything false, challenge me). I would be alone with Socrates, by myself, no one else there. My assumption was that he would immediately have with me the kind of conversation any lover would have with his beloved when they were alone together, and I was delighted. But absolutely nothing like this happened. He would talk to me in his usual way, and after we had spent the day together he would take himself off.

217b

217c

'Next, I invited him to exercise with me and we exercised together; and I hoped that I might at last get somewhere. So, we exercised together and wrestled together many times, when no one else was present. And guess what? I still made no progress. So, having achieved nothing by that manoeuvre, I decided I had to tackle the man head on and not give up now that I had started: I had to know how matters stood. So I sent him an invitation to dinner, exactly as a lover would do who had designs on his beloved. Not even then was he quick to reply, but he did, however, eventually accept. The first time he came he wanted to leave straight after dinner, and on that occasion, feeling embarrassed, I let him go. But the second time I had made my plan, and after dinner I kept him talking far into the night. When he wanted to leave, on the pretext that it was late I successfully pressed him to stay. He prepared to sleep on the couch next to mine, the one he had occupied at dinner, and no one other than the two of us slept in the room.

217d

---

[209] *eironeuomenos.*

'Now, up to this point in my story it has been perfectly all right for   217e
me to tell it to anyone. But you would not have heard from me what is
coming next except that, as the proverb says, wine produces the truth –
never mind the bit about the children[210] – and it seems to me unfair to
pass over in silence a magnificently disdainful act of Socrates when I
have embarked on a eulogy of him. Now, as you know, they say that
anyone who has been bitten by a snake cannot bring himself to describe
what it was like except to those who have had the same experience, for   218a
they are the only ones who will understand and make allowance for
anything the victim did or said in his agony. I too am in that position,
but in my case the bite I have suffered is even more painful, and I
suffered it in the most sensitive part – the heart or the soul or whatever
one is meant to call it. I have been struck and bitten by the things they
talk about in philosophy, and when these get a hold on the soul of a
young man of talent, they bite more cruelly than a snake, and there is
nothing he will not do or say as a consequence. And now when I look at
men like Phaedrus, Agathon, Eryximachus, Pausanias, Aristodemus and   218b
Aristophanes, not to mention Socrates himself and so many others –
you have all shared in the madness and frenzy of philosophy, so you will
all of you hear me out, and I know you will make allowance for what was
done at that time and what is going to be said now. As for you servants
and anyone else who is uninitiated and won't appreciate my story, block
up your ears.

'So, to continue the tale, gentlemen. After the lamp had been put out   218c
and the servants had left the room, I decided that I should no longer
speak equivocally but should say straight out what I was thinking. So I
nudged him and said, "Socrates, are you asleep?"

"No", he replied.

"Do you know what I am thinking?"

"No, what?"

"I think", I said, "that you alone are a worthy lover for me, and you
appear to me to shy away from mentioning the fact. This is how I feel
about it. I consider that it is very foolish of me not to gratify you in this or
in any other way in which you might need help from my resources or from   218d
my friends. For me, nothing is more important than to become as good[211]

---

[210] There was a proverb, 'Truth is revealed by wine and children' (or possibly, 'slaves'; see *pais*).
[211] *beltistos.*

a person as possible, and I think no one would be better fitted to assist me in this aim than you. And I for my part would feel more ashamed at what intelligent men would say if I did not gratify a man such as you than at what the unintelligent public would say if I did gratify you".

'He listened to all this with his very characteristic air of assumed seriousness[212], as he often does, and replied, "My dear Alcibiades, you really must be no ordinary man if what you say about me is actually true 218e and there is in me a certain power through which you might become a better person. You must see in me an irresistible beauty vastly superior to the physical attractions you possess. But if on this basis you are trying to strike a bargain with me and trade your beauty for mine, then your intention is to win a considerable advantage over me. What you are trying to acquire is true beauty in return for apparent[213] beauty, in fact 219a you intend to get 'gold in exchange for bronze'.[214] But look more carefully, dear boy, in case I am actually worthless and you have not noticed. I tell you, mental perception becomes keener when the eyesight starts to fail, and you are still a long way from that"'.

'Hearing all this I replied, "I have said what I have to say, and I have said exactly what I mean. Now you must decide what you think best for 219b you and for me". "That, certainly, is well said", he replied. "At some time in the future you and I will both take stock and do whatever seems best to both of us about this and other matters".

'After this exchange, and having as it were shot my arrows in his direction, I thought I had scored a hit. So without waiting for him to say anything more I got up and putting my heavy cloak around him (it was winter), lay down beside him under his own short cloak and put my arms around him, this truly superhuman[215] and amazing man. This was how 219c I lay all night long. Again, Socrates, you cannot deny that I am telling the truth. Yet despite all that, he completely defeated me, and despised and mocked and insulted[216] my beauty – and in *that* respect I really thought I was something, gentlemen of the jury (I call you that because it is you who will deliver a verdict on Socrates' arrogant behaviour). I swear to you by all the gods and all the goddesses too that when I got up in the

---

[212] *eironikos*; see *eironeuomenos*. [213] See *doxa* in glossary.
[214] A reference to Homer, *Iliad* 6. 234–6, where a Greek warrior exchanges his golden armour for a Trojan's brazen armour ('because Zeus took away his wits').
[215] *daimonios*; see footnote 152. [216] *hubrizein*.

morning after spending the night with Socrates, nothing more had happened than if I had slept with my father or elder brother.

'After that what state of mind do you think I was in? On the one hand I considered that I had been slighted, but on the other I was full of admiration for his character and self-control and manly spirit. I had encountered such a person as I would never have expected to meet for wisdom[217] and steadfastness. Therefore I had no cause to be angry with him or to deprive myself of his company, but neither did I have a way to win him over. I was well aware that he was even less vulnerable to bribery than Ajax to the sword, and he had proved impervious to the one thing I thought might catch him. I was completely at a loss; no one was ever more in thrall to anyone than I was to this man.

'Now all this had already happened when we went on active service together to Potidaea,[218] where we shared the same mess. The first notable thing was that he survived the hardships not only better than I did but better than everyone else. Whenever we were cut off from supplies and compelled to go without food, as happens on campaign, the rest were nowhere when it came to endurance. Yet when provisions were plentiful he was unique in his enjoyment of them; in particular, while he preferred not to drink, when compelled he beat everyone at it. And the most surprising thing of all, no living person has ever seen Socrates drunk. (On this point I rather think he will be put to the test before the night is out.) Anyhow, his endurance of the rigours of winter (for the winters there are severe) was remarkable, especially on one occasion when the frost was at its worst. Everyone else stayed under cover, or if they did venture out they wrapped up to an unusual extent and put on footwear and then wound felt and fleeces round their feet. But in these conditions Socrates went out wearing only the kind of cloak he always wore, and with bare feet, yet he made his way over the ice more easily than the other soldiers did who were wearing shoes, and they looked at him suspiciously, because they thought he was showing them up.

'So much, then, for that episode. There is another story that is worth hearing, "what a thing this was too that he did and endured, stalwart

219d

219e

220a

220b

220c

---

[217] *phronesis.*
[218] A city on the north-east coast of Greece, which revolted from Athenian control in 432 BC. The Athenians besieged it for two years before capturing it.

man",[219] which happened while he was there on campaign. Early one morning, having put his mind to a problem, he stood on the spot thinking about it, and when he could not get anywhere with it he didn't give up but continued to stand there pondering. When it came to midday everyone was beginning to notice, telling each other in amazement that Socrates had been standing there thinking about something ever since daybreak. At last, in the evening after dinner, 220d some of the Ionians carried their sleeping mats outside (by this time it was summer) so that they could sleep in the cool and at the same time watch him to see if he was going to stand there all night. And he did stand there until it was dawn and the sun rose. Then he made a prayer to the Sun and off he went.

'It is only fair to pay my due to him, so if you don't mind I will give you another example from the battlefield. During that battle which resulted in the generals awarding me the prize for valour, it was Socrates 220e and no other who saved my life. He was not prepared to abandon me when I was wounded, and he saved both me and my weapons. In fact, Socrates, I told the generals at the time to give the prize to you, and you cannot fault me for saying this or deny that I am telling the truth. However, the generals had regard to my social standing and wanted to give the prize to me, and you yourself were even keener than they were that I and not you should receive it.

'On another occasion, gentlemen, you should have seen Socrates 221a when the army was in flight from Delium.[220] It happened that I was serving there as a cavalryman and he as a hoplite.[221] The soldiers had already scattered and he was retreating together with Laches[222] when I came across the pair of them, and I immediately encouraged them not to lose heart and I said that I would remain with them. It was here that Socrates made an even greater impression on me than at Potidaea (being on horseback myself I had less to fear). First I noticed how much better 221b he was than Laches at keeping a cool head, and secondly how he was proceeding on his way just as he does here in Athens, exemplifying that

---

[219] Homer, *Odyssey* 4.242 and 271 (slightly misquoted).
[220] In 424 BC the Athenians invaded Boeotia, an independent state bordering their territory to the north-west, and established a stronghold at Delium. When the bulk of the army was returning to Athens it was attacked by the Boeotians and heavily defeated.
[221] A hoplite was a heavily-armed foot-soldier.
[222] An Athenian general at that time; see Glossary of names.

line of yours, Aristophanes,[223] "swaggering and casting sidelong glances", calmly looking sideways as he does at friends and enemies alike, and showing to everyone even at a distance that, if they were thinking of taking this man on, they would have a tough fight on their hands. That was why he and his companion got safely away. Generally speaking the enemy never take on men who behave like this in war, but only go after those who are running away.

'Many other remarkable examples might be cited in praise of Soc- 221c
rates. Although there are some aspects of his behaviour that are similar to other people's, what is so utterly amazing about Socrates is that he himself is completely unlike any other human being who has ever lived, either in the past or in the present. One might, for example, compare Brasidas and others with Achilles, or in the case of Pericles one might 221d
compare him with Nestor or Antenor, and so on; one might make similar comparisons in other cases. But so unusual is our friend here, both in himself and in what he says, that however hard you looked you would never find anyone remotely like him among men of the present or of the past, unless, as I have suggested, you were to compare him, the man and his way of talking, not with any ordinary human being but with the sileni and satyrs.

'For though this is a point I did not mention at the beginning of my speech, it is also Socrates' discourses that are very like those images of Silenus which open up. If you let yourself listen to them they all seem 221e
utterly ridiculous at first hearing, because he wraps everything up in words and phrases which are indeed like the hide of some rude satyr. His talk is all about pack-animals and blacksmiths and cobblers and tanners, and he always seems to be saying the same things in the same words, so that any simple-minded bystander unused to this kind of thing might simply laugh at what he was saying. But if ever you see his 222a
discourse opening up and you get inside it, first you will find that his is the only discourse which has any meaning in it, and then that it is also most divine and contains the greatest number of images of virtue. Moreover, it has the widest application, or, rather, it applies to everything that one should consider if one intends to become fine and good.[224]

'This, gentlemen, is what I have to say in praise of Socrates, but in order not to exclude his faults I have also told you how he insulted me.[225]

---

[223] Aristophanes, *Clouds* 362 (slightly misquoted).   [224] *kalos kagathos.*   [225] *hubrizein.*

And I am not the only one he has treated like this. Charmides, son of
222b   Glaucon, and Euthydemus, son of Diocles have suffered similarly, and
so have many others. They have been deceived into thinking that he
was their lover, but then have found that they were in love with him
instead. So what I say to you, Agathon, is: don't you too be deceived
by this man and like the fool in the proverb have to learn by your own
bitter experience. Learn from us and beware'.

222c   When Alcibiades finished speaking there was laughter at his
frankness, because he seemed to be still in love with Socrates.

'I think you are quite sober, Alcibiades', said Socrates. 'Otherwise
you would never have wrapped up your speech so elegantly in an
attempt to conceal your real motive in saying all this, before, speaking
so casually, you hit the nail on the head at the end. Though you were
222d   pretending otherwise, the reason for your entire speech was to make
Agathon and me quarrel, because you think I ought to love you and
only you, and Agathon ought to be loved by you and by no one else. But
I saw through it, and the plot of this satyr-play, or Silenus-play, of
yours is revealed. My dear Agathon, you must not let him get away with
it. Take care no one drives us apart'.

222e   'I believe you are right, Socrates', replied Agathon. 'I cite as evidence the fact that he took his place on the couch between the two of us
in order to keep us separate. He won't gain anything by it; I shall come
and take the place next to you'.

'Please do', said Socrates. 'Take this place here on my right.'

'Zeus!' exclaimed Alcibiades. 'What I have to put up with from the
man! He thinks he has to get the better of me every single time. My
amazing friend, at the very least let Agathon have the middle place,
between us'.[226]

'Impossible!' declared Socrates. '*You* made a eulogy of *me*, and I in
my turn have to praise the man on my right. So if Agathon is between
us, won't he be praising me again, rather than being praised by me? Be
223a   nice, dear friend, and don't grudge my praising the young man. I have a
strong desire to deliver a eulogy of him'.

---

[226] The seating arrangements on this bottom couch after Alcibiades arrived, were, from left to
right, as follows:
Original placing: Agathon, Alcibiades, Socrates.
Alcibiades proposes: Alcibiades, Agathon, Socrates.
Socrates suggests: Alcibiades, Socrates, Agathon.

'Brilliant!' exclaimed Agathon. 'Alcibiades, I cannot possibly stay here, I absolutely must change places and be praised by Socrates'.

'Here we go again!' said Alcibiades. 'When Socrates is around it is impossible for anyone else to get a look in at attractive young men. And what abundant eloquence he found to make this one here take the place beside him!'

Agathon was getting up to put himself on the right of Socrates when 223b suddenly a crowd of revellers, having found the street door open because a guest was just leaving, made their way straight into the dining room and began to take up places. There was a general commotion and a great deal of wine was forced on everyone and there was no longer any order. Aristodemus said that Eryximachus and Phaedrus and some 223c others went away, and he himself fell asleep and slept for some considerable time (since at that time of year the nights were long). He woke up towards dawn when the cocks were already crowing, and saw that the others were either sleeping or had left, and the only people still awake were Agathon, Aristophanes and Socrates, drinking from a large cup which they passed from left to right. Socrates was still talking to them. Aristodemus said he did not remember most of what was said 223d because he had not been in on the beginning of the conversation and, besides, he kept dropping off to sleep. But the main point was, he said, that Socrates was pressing the others to agree that writing comedy required the same qualities in an author as writing tragedy, and the true tragic poet was a comic poet also.[227] The other two were being urged to reply, but they were getting drowsy and not quite following the argument. Aristophanes fell asleep first and then, when it was already getting light, Agathon. So Socrates, having put them both to sleep, got up and left, and Aristodemus, as usual, followed him. Socrates went to the Lyceum, washed and spent the rest of the day in his customary fashion, and so, towards evening, went home to bed.

---

[227] In Plato's day, a writer of tragedy and a writer of comedy were following separate professions.

Glossary of Greek words

Where appropriate, entries are given in the order (1) verb, (2) noun, (3) adjective; verbs are given in the form of the present infinitive, nouns in the nominative singular, adjectives in the nominative masculine singular. In the transliteration of the Greek letters, Greek υ has been transliterated as u. Unless otherwise stated, footnote numbers refer to the translation. **The meanings given relate to Plato's usage in the Symposium and are not exhaustive.**

agapān	(ἀγαπᾶν) to show devotion or regard, feel affection for. See footnote 51.
agathos	(ἀγαθός) the general adjective for good in the sense of being suited to a desirable purpose or function, or being morally good. The corresponding abstract noun is *arete* and the antonym is *kakos*, bad. In early Greek *agathos* means 'well-born' or, in the political sense, 'aristocratic'. Since the ability to fight well was the attribute of the aristocrat (compare *kalos kagathos*) *agathos* can also mean 'a good fighter', 'brave'. In the plural it often means 'enjoyable material [things]', 'blessings'. The moral sense is often found in the *Symposium*, where 'what is good' sometimes has the abstract sense of 'the good'. If what is good is also attractive, *agathos* comes close in meaning to *kalos*. See also *chrestos*.
aischros	(αἰσχρός) exciting an unfavourable reaction: bad; shameful, dishonourable; unattractive, ugly; wrong (see footnote 55). The antonym is *kalos*.
aischunē	(αἰσχύνη) dishonour, shame; sense of shame, fear of disgrace.
andreia	(ἀνδρεία) manly spirit, bravery; *andreios* (ἀνδρεῖος) manly, brave.
androgunos	(ἀνδρόγυνος) a man-woman. See footnote 96.

64

aporein	(ἀπορεῖν) to be at a loss; *aporia* (ἀπορία) (in a philosophical discussion) the state of being in difficulties, unable to proceed further. This is the state to which Socrates' interlocutors are often reduced as a result of being cross-examined by him. See also *elenchein*.
aretē	(ἀρετή) virtue, goodness, excellence of every kind; since it often denotes non-moral excellence the common translation 'virtue' can sometimes be misleading. *Arete* denotes the several qualities required of a man if he is to be well thought of (see footnote 72); and since it occasionally denotes the reward of excellence it can also mean fame. In early Greek the excellence referred to was commonly courage, a meaning that persisted in Plato's day (compare *andreia*). See also the corresponding adjective *agathos*.
aristos	(ἄριστος) or *beltistos* (βέλτιστος) best, excellent, supreme in goodness; the superlative of *agathos*, good.
aulos	See footnote 18 and **Marsyas** in Glossary of names.
banausos	(βάναυσος) materialistic, relating to the work of artisans, usually in a derogatory sense.
beltistos	see *aristos*.
boulesthai	(βούλεσθαι) to wish, to want (followed by an infinitive).
charizesthai	(χαρίζεσθαι) to do a favour to, to gratify; euphemistically, of the younger male partner in a pederastic relationship, to allow sexual relations, to grant sexual favours.
cheirourgia	(χειρουργία) craft, work done with the hands.
chrēstos	(χρηστός) of persons, good, virtuous, deserving; a word of general commendation.
daimōn	(δαίμων) an unspecified god, particularly a lesser or local deity; divine power generally. See footnotes 151 and 152. *daimonios* (δαιμόνιος) inspired by the divine.
dēmiourgos	(δημιουργός) a craftsman, practitioner, one who has technical skills.
doxa	(δόξα) opinion, what people think, a belief founded on appearance or impression; in Plato often contrasted with knowledge (see *epistasthai*); *doxa* can also mean reputation or fame.
eidos	(εἶδος) form. At 210b the construal 'physical shape' or 'outward form' is commonly accepted; *eidos* also has a philosophical sense where it is associated with the pursuit of the common and essential feature in a variety of things under consideration.

65

eirōneuomenos   (εἰρωνευόμενος) dissimulating, pretending ignorance, pretending not to understand; the adverb *eirōnikōs* (εἰρωνικῶς) has the same meaning. (The noun *eirōneia* (εἰρωνεία), dissimulation, is the source of English 'irony'.)

elenchein   (ἐλέγχειν) to cross-examine so as to refute; *elenchos* (ἔλεγχος) (often spelt in the Latinized form *elenchus*) the procedure of question and answer employed by and associated with Socrates, in which an interlocutor's beliefs are tested by logical argument until it becomes clear that these beliefs are inconsistent and an impasse is reached.

epistasthai   (ἐπίστασθαι) to know; *epistēmē* (ἐπιστήμη) true (i.e. rational) knowledge (compare *doxa*). In the plural, kinds of knowledge, including scientific knowledge. See also *mathēmata*.

epithūmein   (ἐπιθυμεῖν) to want very much, to desire; *epithūmia* (ἐπιθυμία) a strong wish or desire. Compare *eran*.

erān   (ἐρᾶν) to love passionately, be in love with, long for, feel desire for; *ho erōn* (ὁ ἐρῶν) (any)one who loves, lover in a general sense (compare *erastes*); *erōs* (ἔρως) passion, sexual love, desire; also the god Love (see footnote 24).

erastēs   (ἐραστής) lover in the sense of the senior partner in a male homosexual or pederastic relationship.

ergon   (ἔργον) deed, enterprise, activity, occupation, business, work.

erōmenos   (ἐρώμενος) (the) beloved, the younger partner in a male homosexual or pederastic relationship. Compare *paidika*.

erōtica   (ἐρωτικά) literally, things relating to love; translated according to context as the subject of, the study of, the science of, the influence of, or the mystery of love.

eudaimonein   (εὐδαιμονεῖν) to be happy; *eudaimonia* (εὐδαιμονία) happiness, flourishing, well-being; conceptions of *eudaimonia* need not be restricted to subjective feelings such as pleasure, but may involve, for example the (visible) attainment of prosperity, health and success in one's aims (see Introduction p. xvi) see Introduction. The antonym is *kakodaimonia* (κακοδαιμονία), unhappiness, misfortune.

genesis   (γένεσις) coming-into-being, (the process of) generation; origin, parentage, birth.

harmonia   (ἁρμονία) harmony. See footnote 89.

hubrizein   (ὑβρίζειν) to assault, insult, treat with contempt (see footnote 206); *hubris* (ὕβρις) violent abuse, insult; wantonness; *hubristēs* (ὑβριστής) someone sarcastic or insolent. In modern English usage *hubris* generally denotes arrogance leading to disaster.

kakia	(κακία) moral failing; *kakos* (κακός) the general adjective for bad; cowardly. In early Greek, low-born, ugly. The antonym of *kakos* is *agathos*.
kalos	(καλός) fine, beautiful, attractive, good-looking; good, noble; right. *kalōs* (καλῶς, adverb), well. Since what is attractive is likely to seem good to us, *kalos* can be close in meaning to *agathos*, good, though it usually has more of an aesthetic than a moral sense (but see footnote 55). Its antonym is *aischros*, ugly. In Plato 'what is beautiful' sometimes has the abstract sense of 'the beautiful'.
kalos kagathos	(καλὸς κἀγαθός) (in full, *kalos kai agathos*) literally 'fine and good'; it generally describes a man who has the virtues (see *arete*) of an aristocrat or leading citizen, including good looks, intelligence, wealth and social standing.
kosmos	(κόσμος) good order; ornament (see footnote 130); *kosmios* (κόσμιος) orderly; *kosmiōs* (κοσμιῶς, adverb), in an orderly fashion; decently.
mathēmata	(μαθήματα, plural of *mathēma* (μάθημα)) kinds of knowledge, especially scientific knowledge. See also *epistasthai*.
meletē	(μελέτη) practice, exercise; repeating a physical or mental act for the sake of training.
monoeidēs	(μονοειδές) in single form, uncompounded.
mousikē	(μουσική) any art that is the concern of the Muses, especially music or poetry; the arts or culture generally.
neaniskos	(νεανισκός) young man (after the beard has grown).
nomos	(νόμος) a law or rule; convention, custom, principle; *nomimōs* (νομίμως, adverb) lawfully; in accordance with custom.
oikeiotēs	(οἰκειότης) feeling of kinship and affection such as might exist between *oikeioi* (οἰκεῖοι), members of the same family or household.
orthē doxa	(ὀρθὴ δόξα) true or correct belief; right opinion.
ouranios	(οὐράνιος) heavenly. See footnote 53.
paidika	(παιδικά) (virtually synonymous with *eromenos*) beloved boy, the junior partner in a pederastic relationship.
pais	(παῖς) boy, youth, adolescent; the word cannot be applied to a young male after he is fully bearded. It was also used as the appellative of a slave of any age.
peri	(περί, preposition) in the matter of, concerning. See footnote 159.

philein	(φιλεῖν) to love; *philia* (φιλία) (generally non-passionate) love. These words have the most general application of all Greek words for love, describing good relations between people or states, friendship, affection and devotion, even including love between sexual partners. The beloved (*paidika* or *eromenos*) returned his lover's *eros* with *philia*. See footnote 51.
philos	(φίλος) a friend; anyone who is dear to another.
philosophein	(φιλοσοφεῖν) to do philosophy, to be a lover of wisdom, to pursue knowledge or wisdom; *philosophia* (φιλοσοφία) philosophy, the pursuit of knowledge or wisdom (see *sophia*); *philosophos* (φιλόσοφος) a philosopher, a lover of wisdom.
philotimia	(φιλοτιμία) love of honour, i.e. of public recognition; ambition. Also, the object of ambition, i.e. honour, credit.
phronēsis	(φρόνησις) wisdom (sometimes treated as synonymous with *sophia*, and even with *episteme*, knowledge); intelligence, understanding; *phronimos* (φρόνιμος) having intelligent understanding, wise.
phusis	(φύσις) nature, state, condition.
poiēsis	(ποίησις) creation; poetry; *poiētēs* (ποιητής) creator; poet.
psuchē	(ψυχή) (often written *psyche* in English). In Greek popular belief, the principle of life, which leaves the body at death; hence soul or spirit. It is also the principle of thought and feeling, and so can mean mind or consciousness. It is therefore variously translated according as one notion seems to predominate over another.
sophia	(σοφία) In early Greek it denotes knowledge of a skill, an expertise (technical or artistic); in Plato it often means intelligence, knowledge or understanding in a wide sense, of values and actions, such as how to live and behave; hence the common but sometimes misleading translation 'wisdom'. *sophos* (σοφός) expert; skilful; wise, clever, intelligent.
sophistēs	(σοφιστής) a sophist; originally a skilful practitioner of any art or craft (see *sophia*); by Plato's time it had come to denote an itinerant teacher who taught specialist branches of knowledge, in particular the rhetorical skill necessary for swaying large assemblies and for success in political life generally.
sōphrosunē	(σωφροσύνη) good sense, prudence; in a moral sense, temperance, self-control, moderation in the sense of a balance between extremes; *sōphrōn* (σώφρων) sensible, prudent; self-controlled, sober.

technē	(τέχνη) a profession, the practice of an art or craft; a skill; *technikos* (τεχνικός) one who skilfully practises an art or craft, a skilled practitioner.
telos	(τέλος) end, conclusion; sometimes in philosophical use, end in view or aim in the sense of *summum bonum* (Latin, 'maximum good'). It can therefore denote 'that for the sake of which' an action is pursued, or final goal.

Glossary of names

Achilles 10–11, 46, 61   The outstanding hero on the Greek side in the legendary Trojan War (see **Homer**), son of the sea-goddess Thetis and the mortal Peleus. After quarrelling with the Greek commander Agamemnon he withdrew from the fighting until his friend Patroclus was killed by the Trojan hero Hector. He then returned to battle and killed Hector in revenge. Not long after he was killed himself.

Acusilaus 9   A Greek prose-writer and compiler of genealogies who was born towards the end of the sixth century BC and about whom little is known.

Admetus 10, 46   See **Alcestis**.

Aeschylus 10, 10 n. 49   (525–456 BC) The earliest of the three famous Greek tragedians (the others are Sophocles and Euripides). Only seven of his plays survive complete. He may have been the first to make Achilles the lover of Patroclus (rather than the other way round).

Agamemnon 3–4   The commander of the Greek forces in the legendary Trojan War (see **Homer**) and a valiant fighter. His brother Menelaus was the husband of Helen whom the Trojan prince Paris carried off to Troy, thereby initiating the war. Menelaus is referred to at 174c as 'a faint-hearted spearman', but this is a phrase used in a taunt and Homer does not portray him as an inadequate warrior.

70

Agathon vii–viii, xii, xiii, 1–6, 8, 27–32, 33–6, 51–2, 62–3

Described as a *neaniskos* (young man) at 198a, he was perhaps still under thirty, and famous for his good looks, when he won his first poetic competition in 416 BC. After the three great tragedians (see **Aeschylus**) he was the most successful and innovative writer of tragedies, but fewer than forty lines survive. His long-term relationship with Pausanias was well-known. When he left Athens for the court of Archelaus, king of Macedon, where he died probably before 399 BC, Pausanias went with him. Aristophanes in his comedies mocks him for effeminacy and the florid style of his lyrics. See also footnote 4.

Ajax 59

A Greek hero who fought at Troy and was invulnerable not only because of his fighting skills but because he wielded an all-enveloping body-shield.

Alcestis 10–11, 46

In Greek myth, the wife of Admetus, who was granted the possibility of avoiding a fated early death if he could find someone to die for him. Only Alcestis consented, and accordingly died. A version of this story is the subject of Euripides' play *Alcestis*, where she is brought back from death by the hero Heracles.

Alcibiades vii–viii, xxvi–xxviii, 1, 51–63

(451–404 BC) An outstanding personality among his generation at Athens, he came from a rich and politically powerful family. From an early age he dazzled the Athenians with his good looks, wayward talent and brilliant personality, and was soon involved in politics. He was a distinguished army commander during the Peloponnesian War, but his personal ambition led him into acts of betrayal against Athens, and he became widely distrusted. At the time of Agathon's symposium he was at the height of his promise, and in the following year, 415 BC, was appointed one of the three commanders of the (eventually disastrous) Athenian expedition to conquer Sicily, which he had advocated. (See **Sicilian expedition**). At the same time he was implicated, with others of Socrates' acquaintance, in two religious scandals, the profanation of the mysteries and the mutilation of the herms (see **Mysteries** and **Herms**). Thereafter he lived most of his life in exile supporting Athens' enemies, though with interludes when he was regarded with favour by at least some Athenians, and even became a military commander again briefly. His vacillating loyalty baffled the Athenians. In 404 BC he was assassinated abroad in obscure circumstances.

Antenor 61 — See **Nestor**.

Aphrodite 7 n. 24, 8, 11–12, 30, 40 — The Olympian goddess of seduction, sexual love and reproduction, frequently accompanied by Eros (Love, in the sense of powerful sexual desire). The role of Eros in Greek literature cannot easily be distinguished from that of Aphrodite, and Pausanias exploits the idea of their inseparability. The two stories about Aphrodite's birth (see footnote 53) indicate that the Greeks felt her to be a powerful goddess who came to Greece from the East but was under the control of Zeus. She was worshipped widely throughout the Greek world. Her husband was Hephaestus. Her affair with Ares, god of war, was a union of opposites. Pausanias' interpretation of Love as either 'heavenly' or 'common' is found only here.

Apollo 10 n. 42, 23, 31 — An important Olympian god, the son of Zeus and Leto, and a god of many functions. He is the archer-god and the god of music (see **Marsyas**) and sometimes of healing. He also founded the first oracle and can inspire a mortal with the gift of prophecy.

Apollodorus viii, 1–3, 8 — The narrator of the whole of the *Symposium*. Beyond the fact that he was a friend of Socrates we know little more than is revealed at the beginning of this dialogue.

Arcadia 26 n. 109 — The central region of the Peloponnese, where Mantinea was an independent city-state. The whole area was dominated by Sparta.

Ares 30 — The Olympian god of war, whose adulterous union with Aphrodite was witnessed by all the gods (see Homer's *Odyssey* 8. 266–366) after Aphrodite's husband Hephaestus, the god of fire and metal-work, trapped them in a net he had contrived himself.

Aristodemus 2–3, 57, 63 and *passim*   Of Cydathenaeum, a deme (district) of Athens. Apart from his being Apollodorus' source for the *Symposium*, little more is known of him than we are told in the dialogue.

Aristogiton 14   See **Harmodius**.

Aristophanes vii, xii, xiii, 6, 8, 18, 22–7, 51, 57, 61, 63   (c.450–c.386 BC) The most famous Athenian writer of what is known as Old Comedy (comic plays written in verse). Eleven of these plays survive. His plots contain large elements of exaggeration and fantasy, and he parodies or satirises the leading figures of his day, including Agathon and Socrates himself. (See also **Socrates**.)

Asclepius 19   In Homer's *Iliad* Asclepius is a hero and a healer, but by Plato's time he was worshipped as a god and as the founder of medicine. Some families in which medicine was an hereditary skill traced their descent from him, but doctors from other families were also admitted to membership of these 'clans'.

Ate 29   See footnote 118.

Athena 31   The patron goddess of Athens, daughter of Zeus (see **Metis**) and born from his head. She was the virgin protector of the city, a war-goddess and helper of heroes. She was also the goddess of the female craft of weaving, in which she showed the practical intelligence of her mother Metis.

Athens, Athenians, Attica 1, 2, 13–16, 37, 46, 59 n. 218, 60   Athens was the chief city of the state of Attica, which forms the south-east promontory of central Greece. Although Athens was represented in legend as being ruled by kings in mythical times, like other Greek cities she was under the control of aristocrats who remained rich and powerful until their influence was weakened by the reforms of Solon at the beginning of the sixth century BC. The sixth century saw Athens governed by a succession of tyrants (see **Harmodius**), but by the beginning of the fifth century democracy in essentials was established (and lasted until Athens like the rest of Greece lost her independence to Philip of Macedon in 338 BC). In the fifth century

73

BC Athens built a strong navy which from the time of the defeat of the Persians at Salamis in 480 BC (see **Persia**) and for the rest of the century was the most powerful naval force in Greece. Athens' expansionist policy in the middle years of the fifth century roused fears in Sparta and precipitated the Peloponnesian war in 431 BC. (For Athens' unsuccessful attempt to win control of Sicily in 415–413 see **Sicilian expedition**.) The Spartans finally defeated Athens in 404 BC and briefly imposed an oligarchic government, the so-called Thirty Tyrants, with support from some Athenian aristocrats. However, Athens soon regained her democracy and her freedom, if not her former greatness, while Sparta became deeply involved in Persia. The Greek states lost their independence to Philip of Macedon in 338 BC. See also **Sparta**.

aulos 7, 51, 54   See footnote 18 and **Marsyas**.

Boeotia 13   An independent state of central Greece, bordering Attica on the north-west. For the battle of Delium see footnote 220.

Brasidas 61   The outstanding Spartan army commander in the early years of the Peloponnesian war (between Athens and Sparta, 431–404 BC). After he was killed in 422 BC exceptional honours were accorded him.

Chaos 8, 9   'Yawning space'. In the Greeks' mythical cosmogony it was the first created thing, an intangible void beneath the Earth, full of darkness. Ancient authors differ in their interpretation.

Charmides 62   A young and good-looking Athenian aristocrat, one of Socrates' circle of admirers, a few years younger than Alcibiades (b. 451 BC). He was the son of Glaucon and (almost certainly) the brother of Plato's mother, and Plato gave his name as title to one of his own dialogues. Having been named as one in whose house the Eleusinian mysteries had been profaned (i.e. parodied) in 415 BC, he went into exile to avoid the death penalty and suffered the confiscation of his property. Returning later to Athens he sided with the Thirty

Tyrants (see **Athens**) at the end of the Peloponnesian war and was killed in battle against the
democrats in 403.

Codrus 46   A legendary early king of Athens who heard
from an oracle that if he survived an enemy
invasion Athens would be conquered. He therefore contrived his own death, so saving his
country and ensuring that the kingship remained
in his own family for the next three hundred
years or so.

Corybantes 54   See footnote 208. Corybantes were followers of the
orgiastic cult of the Asiatic goddess Cybele, a
goddess of wild nature who was said to cure disease, and whose worship spread widely in the
ancient world.

Cronus 29   In Greek myth, the supreme god of the generation
of gods known as the Titans. These were the
children of Uranus and Gaea (see also footnote
53). Cronus' consort was his sister Rhea. He was
overthrown by his son Zeus, the supreme god of
the generation of Olympian gods, whom the
Greeks worshipped. In Plato's day to call anyone
'older than Cronus (or Iapetus)' meant that they
were very old-fashioned.

Daimon 39   See footnote 151 and Glossary of Greek words.
Delium 60   In south-east Boeotia, the site of a battle between
Boeotians and Athenians in 424 BC. See footnote 220.
Diocles 62   See **Euthydemus**.
Dione 12   A Titan goddess who, according to one story,
became by Zeus the mother of Aphrodite. See
footnotes 53 and 156.
Dionysus 6, 8   Also known as Bacchus. An Olympian god, the son
of Zeus and Semele, the god of wine and ecstasy
and of the surrender of everyday identity, the
patron-god of drama. It was part of his myth that
he was a late-comer to the Olympian pantheon. At
the time of Aphrodite's birthday feast (see 203b)
wine did not exist.
Diotima 37–50   Diotima seems to be represented as an itinerant
'wise woman'. It seems likely that she is a
character invented by Plato. If she had really

existed it is improbable that she would have taught Socrates in the terms of Platonic philosophy that she uses. That she is said to come from Mantinea may be because the Greek word for seer, *mantis*, resembles the place-name. Her own name appears to mean 'honouring (or 'honoured by') Zeus'.

Earth 8–9, 23   See **Gaea**.

Eileithyia 44   The goddess who presided over childbirth, together with one or more of the Fates. The latter decreed the infant's destiny.

Elis 13   A largely rural Greek state in the north-west Peloponnese. The inhabitants were somewhat removed from the political events of the fifth century BC.

Ephialtes 23   In Greek myth, a giant who, with his brother Otus, planned to overthrow the Olympian gods by piling Mount Ossa on Olympus and Mount Pelion on Ossa. They were destroyed by Zeus.

Eros   See **Love** and **Gods**.

Eryximachus vii–viii, xii, xiii, 4, 6–8, 18–22, 26–7, 30, 32, 53, 57, 63   Born c. 448 BC, a doctor and the son of a doctor, Acumenus. He was a friend of Phaedrus, and they were both accused of mutilating the herms.

Euripides 7, 30 n. 127, 33 n. 134   (c. 485–406 BC) With Aeschylus and Sophocles the third of the three great Athenian writers of tragedy. We possess 19 of the 92 plays he is said to have written, and some lines and fragments of the rest. In their questioning of traditional attitudes his plays often reflect the ideas discussed by the intellectuals in Athens in the late fifth century BC. See also **Alcestis**.

Euthydemus 62   A good-looking young man, son of Diocles, a devoted admirer of Socrates. (He is not Euthydemus the sophist after whom one of Plato's dialogues is named.)

Fate 44   In Greek, Moira, Fate in the sense of 'Share', 'Apportionment'; the fate allotted to a person at birth by the goddess (or goddesses) of that name.

Gaea (Earth) 8–9, 23	The primordial goddess who appeared after Chaos, the first created thing. She produced a son Uranus ('Sky' or 'Heaven') and by him had many children whom he forced to remain unborn. She persuaded her youngest child Cronus to overthrow him by castrating him and releasing the children, known as the Titans. The union of Cronus with his sister Rhea produced the race of the Olympian gods.
Giants 23 n. 98	See **Ephialtes**.
Glaucon (1) 2	A friend of Apollodorus. We are not told his father's name or where he lives. For this reason and because the name recurs in Plato's family it has been suggested that this Glaucon would have been recognised as Plato's older brother of that name and Plato would not have needed to explain further. There are some chronological problems with this identification.
Glaucon (2) 62	Father of Charmides.
Gods *passim*	The gods primarily worshipped by the Greeks were the twelve known as the Olympians, a family of gods whose home was on, or in the heavens above, Mount Olympus. For the gods mentioned in the *Symposium* see individual entries for **Aphrodite, Apollo, Ares, Athena, Dionysus, Hephaestus, Hermes** (under **herms**), **Poseidon**, and **Zeus**, the supreme god. Eros (Love) was accepted as a god but was not one of the Olympians. Each of these gods had his or her sphere of interest and influence. Apart from these there were numerous less important deities, who were the subject of myths rather than the object of worship, some of them regarded as older than the Olympians by one or two generations (see **Cronus**). The Greeks generally regarded the Olympians as immortal beings who resembled humans in their desires but were vastly superior to them in size and power, as well as in beauty, wisdom and happiness. See also *daimon* in footnote 151.
Gorgias 32	(c. 485–c. 380 BC) A famous Greek sophist from Leontini in Sicily. From his arrival at Athens in

427 BC he had great influence on the thought and most markedly on the rhetorical style of many of his younger Athenian contemporaries, as is exemplified in Agathon's speech. Features of his style included short balancing clauses, antithesis and assonance, and skilful deployment of ingenious argument. Two short speeches of his, written to dazzle and provoke, still survive. Plato wrote a dialogue named after him in which he figures.

Gorgon 32   In Greek myth the Gorgons were three female monsters whose heads turned to stone anyone who looked at them. One of them, Medusa, was mortal. She was killed by the hero Perseus, who carried off her head to use on his enemies. He then gave it to the goddess Athena, who put it in the centre of her aegis (a kind of over-garment, indestructible and associated particularly with Athena).

Harmodius and Aristogiton 14   'the tyrant-slayers'. Aristogiton was the lover of Harmodius, who was also pursued by Hipparchus, the brother of Hippias, tyrant of Athens. In 514 BC the pair planned to kill both the tyrant and his brother but killed only Hipparchus. They were captured and put to death by Hippias, but were celebrated in popular tradition for having put an end to the tyranny, although it survived until Hippias was driven out of Athens in 510 BC.

Hector 10   In the *Iliad* (see **Homer**), celebrated as the leader of the Trojan army and their bravest hero during the Trojan War. When he kills the Greek warrior Patroclus, the latter's friend Achilles, who has been refusing to fight after a quarrel with Agamemnon, returns to battle to avenge him and kills Hector although he knows that he is thereby fated to be killed himself.

Helios (Sun) 23   In Greek myth, the Sun, personified as a god, son of a Titan (see **Cronus**). The Greeks treated the sun with great respect but did not usually worship him.

Hephaestus 25, 31   The Olympian god of fire and metal-working. Being lame he was something of an exception to the ideal of divine bodily perfection. His wife was

Aphrodite. He was laughed at by the other gods for his lameness but respected for his skill. See **Ares**.

Heracles 7, 51   (The Romans called him Hercules.) Son of Zeus and a mortal woman, Alcmena, he was the most famous of the Greek heroes (though he was of a generation earlier than those who fought at Troy). His exploits (and especially his so-called 'labours', which were imposed on him as punishment for murder, were well-known and he was honoured throughout the Greek world. In Euripides' version of the story of Alcestis he successfully wrestled with Death at her tomb in order to restore her to her family. See also **Prodicus**.

Heraclitus xxi, 19   Of Ephesus in Asia Minor, a philosopher who was active around 500 BC. He is said to have compiled a book of aphoristic sayings which he deposited for readers in the temple of Artemis. These sayings were famously obscure. He thought that the world has an order which depends upon a balance of opposing forces and is in a constant process of change: 'all things are in a state of flux'.

Herms viii   Four-cornered stone or bronze pillars topped with the bearded head of the god Hermes and with a phallus on the front, set up in Athens as road or boundary markers and near public buildings and houses. They were intended to protect and avert evil influences, and were regarded with religious reverence, hence the shock felt when those in Athens were mutilated in 415 BC.

Heroes, heroines 7, 10 n. 48, 11   The children or descendants of unions between gods and humans, larger-than-life characters like Heracles situated in a legendary past. Stories about their lives and exploits dominate Greek myth.

Hesiod 8, 29, 47   With Homer, one of the two great early epic poets of Greece, who lived about 700 BC. His two surviving poems are the *Works and Days*, a didactic poem of advice for farmers, urging a godfearing life of honest hard work, and the *Theogony*, unique in surviving Greek literature as being a systematic account of the origin and genealogy of the Greek gods, together with some of their myths. This work was regarded by the Greeks themselves as being authoritative.

Homer 3, 4, 10 n. 49, 11, 15 n. 70, 23, 29, 30 n. 124, 32, 47, 52 n. 204, 58 n. 214, 60 n. 219

The most famous Greek epic poet, who lived about 750 BC. Homer wrote two verse epics, the *Iliad* and the *Odyssey*. The *Iliad* is the story of an episode in the tenth and last year of the legendary Trojan War. The background is the siege by the Greeks of the city of Troy (also known as Ilium) in Asia Minor (a little south of the Dardanelles), when they were attempting to recapture Helen, the wife of Menelaus; she had eloped with Paris, a Trojan prince. The episode ends with the slaying of the Trojan prince Hector by the Greek hero Achilles. Homer's second epic, the *Odyssey*, deals with the aftermath of the war and the adventurous return to Ithaca from Troy of the Greek hero Odysseus.

Iapetus 29

One of the Titans. See **Cronus.**

Iliad

See **Homer.**

Ionia, Ionians 14 n. 64, 60

Ionia comprised various Greek states along the central west coast of Asia Minor which had been colonised by Greeks from the mainland in about 1000 BC. From 545 BC they were under Persian rule, but by 416 BC, the 'dramatic' date of the *Symposium*, all the Ionian states were subject to Athens, and at the siege of Potidaea (see footnote 216) the Athenians had a large contingent of allies, most of whom were Ionian. However, after 386 BC and at the time Plato was writing the *Symposium*, Ionia was ruled by Persia (see footnote 64).

Isles of the Blest 10, 11

See footnote 48.

King's Peace, The 14 n. 64

A pacification forced upon the warring Greek states in 386 BC by the Persian King Artaxerxes. It decreed that the Ionian Greek cities should be ruled by Persia, but that all other Greek cities should be independent, thus thwarting Athenian

	attempts to regain an empire, and thereby bene-fiting Sparta. See also **Sparta**.
Laches 60	An Athenian general during the Peloponnesian war and friend of Socrates. Plato named one of his dialogues after him. He was killed in 418 BC at the battle of Mantinea.
Love, Eros *passim*	(See footnote 151 and *eran* in glossary.) For the Greeks, and in the *Symposium*, Love is not entirely a human or a natural phenomenon. Some early Greek writers on cosmogony thought that Love was one of the earliest powers to come into existence, together with Chaos and Gaea (Earth). The pre-Socratic philosopher Parmenides also seems to have had Love as a cosmic principle. For the Greeks of Plato's day Love was recognised as a powerful god, but he was not as widely wor-shipped as the Olympian gods (see **Gods**). Mythological stories were not attached to him, and his parentage was a matter of debate. See also **Aphrodite**.
Lyceum 63	A gymnasium and public baths to the east of Athens outside the city wall.
Lycurgus 47	A legendary Spartan of early times, traditionally believed to have created his country's laws as well as their political and military systems. As one of the first law-makers he could be regarded as a benefactor to the whole of Greece.
Mantinea 26 n. 109, 37	A city of Arcadia created by the political unifica-tion of five villages. In 385 BC the Spartans put an end to their democracy and split the city into its original villages (see footnote 109), but they were reunited in 370 BC.
Marsyas 54–5	In Greek myth, a satyr who was the first to play the *aulos* or reeded pipe (see footnote 18). He challenged Apollo, god of music, to a musical contest, but was defeated and flayed alive.
Melanippe 7	A mythical Greek heroine about whom very little is known. She was the subject of two lost plays by Euripides.

Menelaus 3–4	See **Agamemnon**.
Metis 39–40	'Cleverness'; in Greek myth, the first wife of Zeus and the personification of cunning intelligence. When she became pregnant with Athena Zeus swallowed her, because he had been warned that a second child of hers would rule the universe, and thereby he combined supreme power and intelligence within himself. Athena was subsequently born from his head.
Muse, Muses 31	The goddesses of music, dance and literature, and the source of these skills in mortals. They were the daughters of Zeus and Memory. The poet Hesiod is the first to give them their names and number (nine).
Mysteries (1) viii, 54 nn. 207 **and** 208	i.e. mystery religions. Those wishing to join certain religious cults had to be initiated into their secrets or mysteries. The most famous mystery cult at Athens was centred on Eleusis in western Attica, and it was these mysteries that were 'profaned' i.e. parodied in private houses in 415 BC. In some cults a frenzy induced by wild music aided communion with the god.
Mysteries (2) xvii n. 19, xxiii–xxiv, 48	The part of Socrates' speech describing the progress of the lover through various stages in the understanding of beauty until the final stage of seeing absolute Beauty (sometimes called 'the ascent of desire') is expressed by Plato in the language of initiation into the Eleusinian mysteries, first into the Lesser Mysteries (209c–210a) and then into the Higher Mysteries (210a–212b)
Necessity 30 n. 123, 31	Personified as a primordial god.
Nestor 61	In the *Iliad* (see **Homer**), a Greek hero and warrior of great age, famous in later times for wise and persuasive speech, as was the Trojan warrior Antenor.
Odyssey	See **Homer**.
Olympus 54	A mythical musician from Phrygia variously described as the inventor of the *aulos* and of many melodies and as the pupil of Marsyas.

Olympus, Mount	The highest mountain in Greece at the eastern end of a chain that forms roughly the northern boundary of Greece. The Greeks believed that their most important gods, the twelve Olympians, lived on Mount Olympus (or were sometimes thought of as dwelling in the heavens above Olympus), with Zeus's house occupying the summit.
Orpheus 10	In mythical times, a singer and lyre-player of legendary skill. He tried to bring back his dead wife Eurydice from the Underworld by enchanting the powers there, and gained their consent, although in the story related by Phaedrus they released only her phantom. Orpheus broke the condition that he should not look back at her on the upward journey and lost her for ever. He met his own death at the hands of women, a punishment inflicted by the gods, according to Phaedrus, because he tried to enter the Underworld while still alive.
Otus 23	See **Ephialtes**.
Parmenides 9, 29	An important early Greek philosopher from Elea, a Greek colony in South Italy, and born c. 515 BC. In 450 BC he reputedly visited Athens and met Socrates. In the *Symposium* he is mentioned by Phaedrus and Agathon in the context of cosmogony, but we know very little about that aspect of his thought. He expounded his philosophy in a long didactic poem, some parts of which survive. He describes the world in terms of logic and the rules of language rather than in terms of belief.
Patroclus 10	See **Achilles**.
Pausanias vii, xi, xii, xiii, 6, 8, 11–17, 18, 22, 26, 57	Virtually nothing is known of this guest beyond his appearance in Plato. He was the long-term lover of Agathon with whom he left Athens for the court of Archelaus of Macedon.
Peloponnese viii	The southern part of Greece connected with central Greece by the Isthmus of Corinth. The leading state of the Peloponnese in culture and military might was Sparta.

Peloponnesian war
viii

(431–404 BC) A power struggle between democratic Athens, a sea-power which after the Persian wars had developed a Greek empire and acquired considerable influence, and oligarchic Sparta, which had the most efficient land-army of the day and felt threatened by the rise of Athens. Athens' great days ended when she finally capitulated and became for a time the subject-ally of Sparta.

Penia 39, 40

'Poverty', personified as a divinity and according to Socrates the mother of Eros, Love.

Pericles 54, 61

(c. 495–429 BC) From the mid-fifth century until his death Pericles was the most influential politician at Athens, long remembered for his impressive oratory. His imperialistic policy was partly responsible for the outbreak of the Peloponnesian war which brought hardship to the Athenians. He was removed from office in 430 and died (of plague) in 429.

Persia, Persian wars,
47 n. 193

By the fifth century BC the Persian empire extended west as far as the eastern Mediterranean coast and into Thrace, giving the Persians a foothold in Europe. A revolt against Persian rule by Greeks living in Ionia led to a punitive expedition against mainland Greece by the Persian king Darius, which ended in his defeat at the hands of the Greeks at Marathon in 490 BC. In a second invasion in 480 Darius' son Xerxes, after victory at Thermopylae, was defeated at Salamis and Plataea, and the Persians made no further incursion into mainland Greece. Hostilities between Greeks and Persians continued intermittently until a peace treaty in 386 BC, the 'King's Peace', surrendered the Ionian Greek cities to Persian rule (see footnote 64).

Phaedrus vii–viii, xi,
xii, xiii, 6–11, 17, 28,
29, 31, 32, 33, 50, 57,
63

Of the Attic district Myrrhinous, a member of Socrates' circle and friend of Eryximachus. He was one of those accused in 415 BC of profaning (i.e. parodying) the Mysteries, and went into exile, apparently returning to Athens in 404 BC. He died in 393.

Phalerum 1

See footnote 1.

Phoenix 1, 2

Nothing more is known of this guest than is said at 172b.

Plato ix–x, xi n.11; translation footnotes 4, 64, 92, 99, 109, 137, 151, 201, 227

(c.424–348 BC) Son of Ariston and Perictione, Plato was from a rich and politically important family. His older brothers Adimantus and Glaucon associated with Socrates, who exerted a powerful influence on Plato. At some point he renounced a career in politics in favour of philosophy. The story goes that he was invited to the court of Dionysius I, tyrant of Syracuse, who became angry when Plato spoke out too freely and had him seized and put up for sale as a slave. His friends paid the price and freed him. Returning to Athens he founded a mathematical and philosophical school, the Academy (on land dedicated to the Greek hero Academus). Here he wrote many philosophical works which still survive, in the form of dialogues in which Socrates figures largely but he himself not at all. Thus the ideas and arguments in these works are never represented as Plato's own. In 367 BC the young Aristotle, the future philosopher, came to the Academy to study and remained there until Plato's death in 348. Plato was buried in the Academy.

Polymnia 20

'She of many hymns', one of the Muses.

Poros 39–40

'Resource', personified as a divinity.

Poseidon 53

An important Olympian god, the god of the sea and also of earthquakes and horses. Alcibiades' oath 'by Poseidon' at 214d is unique in Plato but is found in Athenian comedy.

Potidaea 59, 60

A city on the north-east coast of Greece, a colony of Corinth which became a subject-ally of Athens. It revolted in 432 BC but was retaken by Athens in 430 BC after a siege.

Prodicus 7

From the Aegean island of Ceos, a sophist of great reputation in Athens in the late fifth century BC. He was the author of a well-known allegory in which the hero Heracles (Hercules) has to choose between two paths, one of virtue and the other of vice, and chooses virtue.

Satyrs, Sileni (sing., **Silenus**) 53–4, 55, 61

Mythical male inhabitants of the wild countryside, lewd, drunken and mischievous, the counterpart of nymphs with whom they make up the attendants of Dionysus, the god of wine. They were portrayed as snub-nosed and with protuberant eyes (like Socrates), and sometimes with animal features such as horse-tails.

Selene (Moon) 23 The Greek moon-goddess, associated with women and often with magic. Many different genealogies were ascribed to her, and some ancient writers stated that she was bisexual.

Sicilian expedition viii In 415 BC, during the Peloponnesian war, the Athenians were persuaded largely by Alcibiades to send an expeditionary force to Sicily, with the ultimate hope of controlling the island and the surrounding sea-ways. The expedition set sail in an atmosphere of anxiety caused by religious scandals (see **Mysteries** and **Herms**), and within two years had been defeated by the Spartans and their allies with great loss of life and resources. This failure contributed to Athens' final defeat by Sparta in the war.

Sileni, Silenus See **Satyrs**.

Sirens 55 Enchantresses who, in the *Odyssey* (see **Homer**), lure sailors to their death by their beautiful singing. Odysseus stopped the ears of his crew with wax so that they did not hear the song.

Socrates *passim*; see especially vii, xiii–end, 33–6, 37–50 (469–399 BC) The best-known intellectual figure at Athens in the second half of the fifth century BC, complex and enigmatic. He exerted considerable influence on the rich young men, future politicians, with whom he associated, although he never claimed to teach, nor did he accept fees, unlike the sophists whom he superficially resembled in his apparent questioning of accepted beliefs. The oracle at Delphi declared that no one was wiser than Socrates, which Socrates interpreted as meaning that he alone was aware of his own ignorance. A stonemason by trade, he was married to Xanthippe and had three sons. He fought with distinction as a hoplite (a heavily-armed foot-soldier) in three famous engagements in the Peloponnesian war. He had a reputation for being impervious to pleasures and hardships alike. He enjoyed good company, food and wine, but went about bare-footed and remained relatively poor. He did not play an active role in politics but when he was required on two occasions to act illegally he refused. He claimed that a 'divine sign' intervened to prevent him, as on some other occasions. Many of the young men in his circle who became prominent in politics turned against democracy (see **Alcibiades** and **Athens**), and it seemed to many citizens that his influence upon these men had been bad and was partly responsible for Athens' defeat in the Peloponnesian war. Perhaps because of this and also as a result of the hostile mockery of the comic playwright Aristophanes, Socrates was tried and convicted of impiety and of corrupting the youth, and was condemned to death. Escape abroad, though possible, would have been against the law, and so he remained in prison and drank the hemlock. Socrates wrote nothing himself. Many of his contemporaries, not only Plato, wrote dialogues in which he figured prominently, but most of these accounts have been lost. His interest was in ethical questions concerning the nature of virtue and of the good and happy life. He believed in the primacy of knowledge and the importance of definitions, but he is not represented as expounding views of his own. Rather he questions the views of others by his procedure of question and answer which has come to be known as the elenchus (see *elenchein* in Glossary of Greek words). Although the result of his enquiries seems in fact to have been negative, the example of his life and above all of his death have made him a paradigmatic philosopher.

Solon 47   (active in the early sixth century BC) A highly-regarded political figure at Athens, a social reformer and legislator who wrote about his work in poetry, some of which survives. Later Athenians commonly referred to all their laws as 'the laws of Solon'.

Sophocles 30 n. 123

(c. 496–405 BC) With Aeschylus and Euripides one of the three great Athenian writers of tragedy. Only seven of his plays survive complete.

Sparta, Spartans 13, 26, 47

Sparta was the chief city of Laconia and the name is commonly given in English to the whole city-state, situated in the south-east Peloponnese. By the beginning of the fifth century BC Sparta was the leading military power in Greece and played a vital part in defeating the Persians in the land-battles of 490 and 480 BC. However, the Athenian navy had also played a decisive role and Athens emerged from the Persian wars with enhanced prestige which she used to increase her power and influence. By 431 BC Sparta, feeling threatened by Athenian imperialism, entered into war with Athens (the Peloponnesian war) from which she eventually emerged victorious in 404. In 400 she embarked on an initially successful war against Persia, but at home she had to deal with a coalition of hostile Greek states, including Athens. In 386 Sparta was the chief beneficiary of the so-called 'King's Peace', imposed by the Persian king, according to which the Greek cities on the west coast of Asia Minor fell under Persian rule again, but all other Greek cities were to be self-governing. By this decree Athens was prevented from building up an empire again, but Sparta was free to lead a voluntary alliance of Peloponnesian states.

Spirit

See **Daimon.**

Sun

See **Helios.**

Thetis 10

In Greek myth, a sea-goddess fated to bear a son more powerful than his father. Zeus gave her in marriage to a mortal hero Peleus, and their son was Achilles.

Titans

See **Cronus** and **Zeus.**

Trojan War

See **Homer.**

Underworld 10, 26

See footnote 48.

Urania 20

('Heavenly One') the name of one of the Muses.

Uranus 11

See **Cronus, Gaea** and footnote 53.

Zeus 12 n. 53, 23, 24, 26, 31, 38, 39, 43, 58 n. 214, 62

In Greek myth and religion, the ruler of the Olympian gods, the son of the Titans Rhea and Cronus, whom he overthrew. Another Titan, Hera, was his wife, and he was the father of most of the powerful Olympian gods. After the overthrow of Cronus, Zeus and his brothers divided the universe between themselves by casting lots, and Zeus obtained the heavens as his domain. His weapon, the thunderbolt, was wielded only by him and symbolised his invincible power over gods and men. See also **Gods** and **Metis**.

Index of subjects

adultery 25
appearance (contrasted with reality) 33, 55, 58
ascent of desire xx, xxiv, xxvi, 48–50
astronomy 21
athletics xvii, 42

beauty, beautiful xii, xiii, xiv, xix n. 21,
    xx–xxii, xxiii, xxiv, xxvi, 3, 10, 18,
    28, 30, 31, 32, 36, 38, 41, 43–4,
    47–50, 51, 56, 58
belief 37
(the) beloved viii, 9, 11, 13–14, 15–17, 25–6,
    50, 56
birth, giving 31, 43–4, 47–8, 49–50
body 12, 13, 15, 18–19, 22–4, 30, 44–6,
    47, 48–9
boy, youth, young man 16, 25, 48, 49, 50, 63
bravery see courage

character x, xxviii, 16, 17, 29
cicadas 24
comedy 26, 63
conception 24, 39, 44, 47
contemplation xiii, xx, xxii, xxiv, xxv
copulation 45
courage, bravery, valour xiii, 9–11, 25, 30, 50, 60
cowardice 9, 14
craft, craftsman 31, 39, 42, 47, 54

dating of Symposium vii n. 3, 2 nn. 4, 6,
    26 n. 109
democracy 14 n. 66
desire ix, x, xii, xiii, xiv, xx, xxii, xxiv–xxv, 18,
    24, 25–6, 31, 34–6, 40–6
disease 18–19, 21, 37, 43
divination xiii, 21, 31, 39

dreams 5
drinking, drunkenness 6–7, 39, 51–3, 59, 63
dualism 18–21

education ix, xxvi, xxviii, 14 n. 65, 17, 20, 47
elenchus x, 33–6
encomium x
excellence xi–xii, xiii, xxiii–xxiv, xxv, xxviii,
    11, 16–17, see also virtue

fame see honour
fine and good 40, 61
Forms, Ideas xx–xxii, xxv, xxviii

generation 45–6
(the) good xvii–xviii, xxiii–xxiv, 36, 41, 42–4
(the) good life ix–x, xxviii, 50, see also
    happiness
gratify, grant sexual favours to 13–17, 18,
    20, 21, 58
gymnasia, gymnastics 14, 19

happiness ix–x, xi, xiii, xiv–xviii, xx, xxiii, xxv,
    11, 21, 26, 28, 38, 41, 42, 46
harmony 19–21
health 18–19, 20–1
heavenly love 11–13, 17, 20
heroes see Glossary of names
hiccups 18, 22
historical background viii, xxvii
homosexuality
    female 25
    male viii–ix, xxvi, 12
    and passim, see also pederasty
honour xi, xxiv, xxv, xxvii–xxviii, 9–11,
    46–8, 50

Ideas *see* Forms
ignorance 33, 37, 38, 40, 41; Socratic ignorance 55, 56, 58
immortality xviii, 38, 44, 45−8, 50
initiation 48, 54
injustice 30
insolence (*hubris*) 6 n. 16, 23, 58, *see also* irony, sarcasm
inspiration 10, 12, 20 n. 92, 47 n. 192
irony, sarcasm 6, 56 n. 209, *see also* insolence

justice 17, 21, 47

knowledge xx−xxii, xxiii n. 26, 19, 20, 21, 38, 40, 45, 46, 49, 50

law 13−14, 30, 48
love, lover *passim*

magic 39, 40
marriage 25, 47
medicine xii, xiii, 6, 18, 19, 31
moderation, moderate 21, 23, 47
money 2, 15−16, 17, 42, 46
music 19−20, 54−5
mysteries xvii n. 19, *see also* Glossary of names
myth 10, 23, 32, *see also* **Gods** and **Heroes** in Glossary of names

necessity 29, 30 n. 123, 31

opinion 37
oracles *see* **Socrates** in Glossary of names, *see also* divination, magic

pederasty 10−18 and *passim*
personification 7 n. 24, 39 n. 157
philosopher, philosophy x, xiii, xvii, xxvi, 2, 14, 16 n. 73, 41, 42, 57
piety, impiety 21
poetry xiii, 42
poets 7, 8−9, 19, 29, 30, 42, 47−8, 63
    see for individuals Glossary of names
politics, politician xiii, 15, 16, 25, 55

prayer 6, 60
pregnancy xix, 39, 44−8
priests 39
procreation 39, 44-45
prophecy *see* divination

rhetoric 17
riches, rich *see* wealth
right and wrong 12−17, 19

sacrifices 2, 21, 22, 23, 31, 37, 39
sarcasm, *see* irony
satyrs and sileni *see* Glossary of names
setting vii−viii
seer *see* divination
sex *passim*
shame 9, 16, 17, 25, 32, 55, 56, 58
sileni, *see* **Satyrs** in Glossary of names
sober 52, 53, 62
sophists 7, 40, 46
soul xi, xii, 10, 12, 15, 18, 29, 44−8, *see also* character
speeches *see*, Glossary of names, Phaedrus, Pausanias, Eryximachus, Aristophanes, Agathon, Socrates
spirit 39
symposium vii−ix, 4−6

tallies 25, 26
theatre 27−8
tyranny 14

virtue (*arete*) xii, xix, xxii, 9, 16 n. 72, 30, 47, 48, 50, 61, *see also* excellence

wealth x, 2, 9, 17, 35, 40, 57
wisdom x, xi, xii, xiv, xxviii, 5, 16−17, 30, 31, 37, 40, 41, 43, 47, 49, 51, 59
women 7, 10, 12, 13, 25, 26, 46
wrestling 56

young man *see* boy
youth *see* boy

Cambridge Texts in the History of Philosophy

Titles published in the series thus far

Aquinas *Disputed Questions on the Virtues* (edited by E.M. Atkins and Thomas Williams)

Aquinas *Summa Theologiae, Questions on God* (edited by Brian Davies and Brian Leftow)

Aristotle *Nicomachean Ethics* (edited by Roger Crisp)

Arnauld and Nicole *Logic or the Art of Thinking* (edited by Jill Vance Buroker)

Augustine *On the Trinity* (edited by Gareth Matthews)

Bacon *The New Organon* (edited by Lisa Jardine and Michael Silverthorne)

Boyle *A Free Enquiry into the Vulgarly Received Notion of Nature* (edited by Edward B. Davis and Michael Hunter)

Bruno *Cause, Principle and Unity* and *Essays on Magic* (edited by Richard Blackwell and Robert de Lucca with an introduction by Alfonso Ingegno)

Cavendish *Observations upon Experimental Philosophy* (edited by Eileen O'Neill)

Cicero *On Moral Ends* (edited by Julia Annas, translated by Raphael Woolf)

Clarke *A Demonstration of the Being and Attributes of God and Other Writings* (edited by Ezio Vailati)

Classic and Romantic German Aesthetics (edited by J.M. Bernstein)

Condillac *Essay on the Origin of Human Knowledge* (edited by Hans Aarsleff)

Conway *The Principles of the Most Ancient and Modern Philosophy* (edited by Allison P. Coudert and Taylor Corse)

Cudworth *A Treatise Concerning Eternal and Immutable Morality* with *A Treatise of Freewill* (edited by Sarah Hutton)

Descartes *Meditations on First Philosophy*, with selections from the *Objections and Replies* (edited by John Cottingham)

Descartes *The World and Other Writings* (edited by Stephen Gaukroger)

Fichte *Foundations of Natural Right* (edited by Frederick Neuhouser, translated by Michael Baur)

Fichte *The System of Ethics* (edited by Daniel Breazeale and Günter Zöller)

Hamann *Philosophical Writings* (edited by Kenneth Haynes)

Heine *On the History of Religion and Philosophy in Germany and Other Writings* (edited by Terry Pinkard, translated by Howard Pollack-Milgate)

Herder *Philosophical Writings* (edited by Michael Forster)

Hobbes and Bramhall on Liberty and Necessity (edited by Vere Chappell)

Humboldt *On Language* (edited by Michael Losonsky, translated by Peter Heath)

Hume *Dialogues Concerning Natural Religion and Other Writings* (edited by Dorothy Coleman)

Hume *An Enquiry Concerning Human Understanding* (edited by Stephen Buckle)

Kant *Anthropology from a Pragmatic Point of View* (edited by Robert B. Louden with an introduction by Manfred Kuehn)

Kant *Critique of Practical Reason* (edited by Mary Gregor with an introduction by Andrews Reath)

Kant *Groundwork of the Metaphysics of Morals* (edited by Mary Gregor with an introduction by Christine M. Korsgaard

Kant *Metaphysical Foundations of Natural Science* (edited by Michael Friedman)

Kant *The Metaphysics of Morals* (edited by Mary Gregor with an introduction by
  Roger Sullivan)
Kant *Prolegomena to any Future Metaphysics* (edited by Gary Hatfield)
Kant *Religion within the Boundaries of Mere Reason and Other Writings* (edited by Allen Wood
  and George di Giovanni with an introduction by Robert Merrihew Adams)
Kierkegaard *Fear and Trembling* (edited by C. Stephen Evans and Sylvia Walsh)
La Mettrie *Machine Man and Other Writings* (edited by Ann Thomson)
Leibniz *New Essays on Human Understanding* (edited by Peter Remnant and Jonathan
  Bennett)
Lessing *Philosophical and Theological Writings* (edited by H.B. Nisbet)
Malebranche *Dialogues on Metaphysics and on Religion* (edited by Nicholas Jolley and
  David Scott)
Malebranche *The Search after Truth* (edited by Thomas M. Lennon and Paul J. Olscamp)
Medieval Islamic Philosophical Writings (edited by Muhammad Ali Khalidi)
Medieval Jewish Philosophical Writings (edited by Charles Manekin)
Melanchthon *Orations on Philosophy and Education* (edited by Sachiko Kusukawa,
  translated by Christine Salazar)
Mendelssohn *Philosophical Writings* (edited by Daniel O. Dahlstrom)
Newton *Philosophical Writings* (edited by Andrew Janiak)
Nietzsche *The Antichrist, Ecce Homo, Twilight of the Idols and Other Writings* (edited by
  Aaron Ridley and Judith Norman)
Nietzsche *Beyond Good and Evil* (edited by Rolf-Peter Horstmann and Judith Norman)
Nietzsche *The Birth of Tragedy and Other Writings* (edited by Raymond Geuss and Ronald
  Speirs)
Nietzsche *Daybreak* (edited by Maudemarie Clark and Brian Leiter, translated by
  R.J. Hollingdale)
Nietzsche *The Gay Science* (edited by Bernard Williams, translated by Josefine Nauckhoff)
Nietzsche *Human, All Too Human* (translated by R.J. Hollingdale with an introduction by
  Richard Schacht)
Nietzsche *Thus Spoke Zarathustra* (edited by Adrian Del Caro and Robert B. Pippin)
Nietzsche *Untimely Meditations* (edited by Daniel Breazeale, translated by
  R.J. Hollingdale)
Nietzsche *Writings from the Late Notebooks* (edited by Rüdiger Bittner, translated by
  Kate Sturge)
Novalis *Fichte Studies* (edited by Jane Kneller)
Plato *The Symposium* (edited by M.C. Howatson and Frisbee C.C. Sheffield)
Reinhold *Letters on the Kantian Philosophy* (edited by Karl Ameriks, translated by James
  Hebbeler)
Schleiermacher *Hermeneutics and Criticism* (edited by Andrew Bowie)
Schleiermacher *Lectures on Philosophical Ethics* (edited by Robert Louden, translated by
  Louise Adey Huish)
Schleiermacher *On Religion: Speeches to its Cultured Despisers* (edited by Richard Crouter)
Schopenhauer *Prize Essay on the Freedom of the Will* (edited by Günter Zöller)
Sextus Empiricus *Against the Logicians* (edited by Richard Bett)
Sextus Empiricus *Outlines of Scepticism* (edited by Julia Annas and Jonathan Barnes)

Shaftesbury *Characteristics of Men, Manners, Opinions, Times* (edited by Lawrence Klein)

Adam Smith *The Theory of Moral Sentiments* (edited by Knud Haakonssen)

Spinoza *Theological–Political Treatise* (edited by Jonathan Israel, translated by Michael Silverthorne and Jonathan Israel)

Voltaire *Treatise on Tolerance and Other Writings* (edited by Simon Harvey)

CPSIA information can be obtained
at www.ICGtesting.com
Printed in the USA
LVHW050136271222
735866LV00006B/727